The
CARIBOU
HOTEL

Hauntings, hospitality, a hunter, and the parrot

BY JOHN FIRTH

Copyright@John Firth 2019 The Caribou Hotel: Hauntings, hospitality, a hunter and the parrot
Publisher: John Firth/ Caribou Hotel
Whitehorse, Y.T., Canada

ISBN: 978-0-9867603-1-0

Cover and interior design and layout, maps, schematics: Mike Rice - Catalyst Communications, Whitehorse, Yukon
Cover art: Front: Caribou Hotel by Ted Harrison (used with permission from Wingate Arts Limited),
Back: untitled by Anna Gertrude Scott (used with permission from Anne Morgan)
Sketch artist for chapters 1, 27 and 28: Daphne Mennell.
Editing: Erin McMullan, Ucluelet, B.C.
See page 243 for a complete list of photo credits

For permission to reproduce the information in this publication for commercial redistribution or for additional copies, please contact:

John Firth
Email: johnfirth@hotmail.ca
Website: johnfirth.ca

Although every effort has been made to ensure the information in this book was correct at press time, the author/publisher do not assume and hereby disclaim any liability to any party for any loss, damage or disruption caused by errors or omissions, whether such errors or omissions result from negligence, accident, or any other cause.

The Caribou Hotel acknowledges the support of the Yukon Historic Resources Fund for their assistance in this publication.

Printed in Canada by Canam Books, Montreal, Quebec

BOOKS BY JOHN FIRTH

Yukon Challenge/republished as Yukon Quest:
The 1000-mile dog sled race through the Yukon and Alaska

River Time: Racing the Ghosts of the Klondike Rush

One Mush: Jamaica's Dog Sled Team

Yukon Sport: An Illustrated Encyclopedia

Better Than A Cure: One Man's Journey to Free the World of Polio (with Ramesh Ferris)

Whitehorse: An Illustrated History (with nine other writers)

John Firth is an award winning writer who lives in Whitehorse, Yukon.

Bessie Geraldine Gideon

THE CARIBOU HOTEL

SE "Tutshi" at Carcross

"All of us older Yukoners - we can remember when the hotels in these small towns did embody the heart of the community and who was running them really had a huge impact on our lives."

DAPHNE MENNELL,
CARCROSS ARTIST,
2017

THE CARIBOU HOTEL   6

TABLE
OF
CONTENTS

TABLE OF CONTENTS
CONTINUED

Archie meets Bessie Gideon

Chapter 1

A NIGHT VISITOR

"Agnes? What are you doing here?"

Archie Lang had gone to bed alone. He had no guests in the hotel on this night. Now he had been jolted out of his sleep to find a woman standing in the door to his second-floor bedroom.

Seen through his sleep-addled eyes she looked like his housekeeper – Agnes Johns. But what was Agnes doing here in the middle of the night? He glanced at the luminous dial on his alarm clock.

"Agnes. It's three-thirty in the morning. Is there something wrong?"

The woman moved closer to the bed. She might be Agnes, but now Archie wasn't so sure. Her grey hair indicated she was about the right age – in her sixties, about 40 years older than he – but that's where the similarity ended.

She wore what he thought of as "a Mother Hubbard" dress – a simple, gingham dress that tied at the back. On her head was a hair net. On her wrist was a watch held on by an expandable band – something common for men to wear in 1969, but not women.

It was her eyes that unnerved him. Cold, empty, unblinking. It was as if she was staring straight through him.

Archie, remembering he wore nothing under the covers and feeling an involuntary chill under her gaze, pulled the duvet up closer to his chin, peeked over to where his housecoat was draped over a chair, then back at her.

He was still new at this, having just signed a one-year lease to operate the Caribou Hotel a few months earlier. He still wasn't sure what was going to happen from day to day, being a carpenter by trade and not an hotelier, but an uninvited guest hanging around in his room in the middle of the night was certainly not what he expected. He stopped talking, unsure of where this was going.

The woman stood there for a few more minutes staring back at him, then abruptly turned, crossed the floor and went out the door. Archie jumped up, grabbed his housecoat and followed her but when he reached the hallway she was nowhere to be seen. He glanced to his right but the plywood that blocked off access to the third floor was still intact. The only place she could have gone, he reasoned, was downstairs to the beer parlour or the café.

He crept slowly down the creaking stairs with its threadbare carpeting and wooden handrails worn by generations of hands and children sliding down them. Halfway down, he peered around the corner but didn't see anything in the front entryway – all the time muttering to himself in that way nervous people do.

"She's not here," he said, turning on the lights in the empty beer parlour. The mounted moose heads on the wall simply stared silently back at him.

"Hello," he called to the café and the kitchen, "Agnes, are you here?" neither expecting a reply nor getting one.

As he passed the front door he tested it to see if it was still locked. It was. Same with the back door. And the windows. The parrot's cage was still covered. "Did you see her Polly?" he asked. There was no movement or sound within – but then there's not much that can disturb a 120-year old bird who sleeps most of the time anyway.

The staircase down which Mrs. Gideon walked

By then, almost all the lights in the hotel were on and there was no sign of anyone else in the place.

He wondered if she had gone into the basement so he grabbed a flashlight from behind the bar and started down the stairs, pausing apprehensively on each step to peer into the gloom below him. It was pierced only by his beam of light and the occasional flicker of red from the wood-burning furnace. Still there was no answer to his quavering calls.

There was no sign of her in the space under the hotel – it could hardly be called a basement with its sand floor and sagging beams and plumbing pipes suspended ominously above his head. The hotel was cold at the best of times and he still had a chill from her presence so he plucked wood from the pile in the corner and hurled it into the furnace, hoping the extra heat would to warm him up. Then he climbed back up through the hotel to his room – all the while checking over his shoulder and wondering if he had somehow missed a clue as to where she had vanished to.

Basement below Caribou Hotel where the search ended.

There had been something off about the search for Agnes but he couldn't quite put a finger on it. It was a long time before he finally dozed off.

In the morning when he woke up it occurred to him what it was he heard – or rather, didn't hear – the night before. He realized it was that absence that had bothered him almost as much as her eyes.

"She couldn't have beat me down the stairs," he muttered to himself, thinking about the creaking stairs, the doors too tight to be closed quietly, and the windows that rattled with any kind of disturbance. "She couldn't have gone down the stairs or out the door without making some noise – and I didn't hear anything."

When he pulled the cover off Polly's cage the aged parrot didn't seem to think there was anything unusual afoot. He ruffled his feathers and swore at Archie just as he did every morning.

That morning Agnes's son Howard turned up at the hotel for his first coffee of the day.

"You know," Archie said to him, "Your mother was wandering around here at about three-thirty this morning. I was wondering what was going on."

"My mother?!" replied Howard, "My mother's in Stewart Crossing visiting my sister Shirley. She's not here. She's been gone for two weeks."

"You're kidding."

"No."

"Well, I saw her...or I guess I did. I saw somebody."

One of the next customers through the café door was Agnes's brother, retired outfitter Johnnie Johns — for over 50 years a daily fixture in the hotel.

Archie told him the story.

"Describe her to me," said Johnnie. Archie did.

The retired hunting guide was pensive for a moment then quietly said, "You just described Mrs. Gideon. The dress. The hairnet. I don't remember the watch but everything else is just like she used to dress. Wore that dress when she was cooking. She was a severe-looking woman. She died in that room in 1933."

Archie had heard about the Caribou being haunted but had dismissed it as just a tale to scare children.

"My room!?"

Johnnie nodded, "Might even have been the same bed."

Bessie Gideon had been the manager then owner of the Caribou Hotel for 25 years. About the only ones around who were still alive and might remember her were the parrot, Polly — who had arrived in 1918 — and Johnnie, who would have known her when he was a young man.

Carcross was a small town and word of Archie's night-time encounter got around town quickly.

He had one of the busiest days he would experience during his year as manager of the hotel. A steady stream of customers turned up for a coffee in the restaurant or a drink in the bar and all they wanted to talk about was Mrs. Gideon.

"I saw the ghost and that was pretty important," Archie remembered in 2017, "so everybody in town had to come and talk to me and hear the story."

In the late hours of the evening, when even the bar crowd was thinning out, Archie made a decision.

"You know," he said to one of his customers, Carl Wetherall, "I think I'm going to move into room seven. I don't really want to spend the night with Mrs. Gideon again."

Carl nodded in silent agreement but another customer, "Shorty" Schroder, spoke up.

"You'd better say hello to Ken while you're up there," he said.

"Who's Ken?"

"He died in room seven in 1957."

"He was a nasty guy," chipped in Carl.

"I decided to stay with Mrs. Gideon," Archie recalled. "She was a ghost but at least she wasn't a nasty guy like Ken... sad to say, I never saw her again."

Chapter 2

THE YUKON HOTEL

It was immediately obvious that John Barrett was one of those stampeders who mines the miners rather than the gold when he walked into Bennett, BC late in the winter of 1897-98. Included in his outfit was a substantial supply of alcohol and the first thing he did was set up a tent beside the Dawson Hotel and open a wholesale liquor outlet.

For the thousands of stampeders, who had spent much of the previous winter lugging their outfits from tidewater at Dyea, Alaska, over the coastal mountains to the tent town on the southern tip of Bennett Lake, the devil's drink wasn't the "ticket to sulphurdom" as the Temperance movement claimed. For them it was heaven on earth after months of depriving themselves of the pleasures of the flesh while slogging through some of North America's most brutal terrain under the worst conditions imaginable – all the while hoping and praying they would reach the Klondike Gold Fields in time to make their fortune.

Even after arriving in Bennett most spent endless, tortuous days whipsawing logs into boards with which to build a boat. Some had

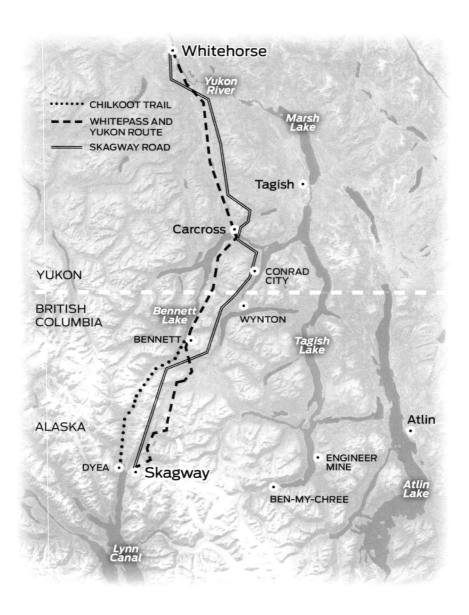

Whitehorse

- ······· CHILKOOT TRAIL
- ━ ━ ━ WHITEPASS AND
  YUKON ROUTE
- ——— SKAGWAY ROAD

Yukon River

Marsh Lake

Tagish

Carcross

YUKON

CONRAD CITY

BRITISH COLUMBIA

Bennett Lake

WYNTON

BENNETT

Tagish Lake

ALASKA

Atlin

DYEA   Skagway

ENGINEER MINE

Atlin Lake

BEN-MY-CHREE

Lynn Canal

Yukon Hotel as a tent in Bennett 1898

enough money to buy boards from one of the six sawmills in the area to construct their boats. Once built, the boats were parked on the lakeshore just beyond the reach of the ice and everyone then had to sit in their small canvas tents, crammed with provisions, bedding, and firewood, waiting for winter to end.

To pass the time the thousands of men – women were rare in Bennett – played baseball games and chess, held tug-o-wars and public speaking competitions, caught up on current affairs by attending public readings of month-old newspapers brought in over the Chilkoot Trail, and attended lectures by one of the many scientists or philosophers among their number.

For those who wanted something a bit more daring they could frequent the growing number of tent hotels down by the waterfront and along Bennett's Main Street where they could drink, gamble or spend time with the few "Ladies of Liberty" who worked there. John provided the gambling and drinking establishments with their alcohol.

A few of the hotel and restaurant owners were starting to construct log cabins to replace their original tent structures. They were usually rough two story buildings – the main floor being a single room in the middle of which there was a cooking stove covered with pots and pans. Long tables and benches lined the walls. The grub wasn't very good and the grog was weak. The floor was covered with mud from the men's boots, which found its way onto the benches, the tables, and into the food. In the evenings, light was provided by candles stuck into the necks of bottles.

The top floor, accessible by a ladder, was also a single room. Hotel guests would find a spot on the overcrowded floor on which to spread their blanket and go to sleep. The space reeked from the stench of the unwashed and the odour of greasy food, stale booze, and cigar smoke wafting up from below. The bare boards almost as filthy as the floor of the restaurant below them but there were few alternatives in a stampede town.

Whether Frank Turner and Thomas Geiger arrived in town to seek gold or fleece their fellow stampeders isn't clear. Neither is whether or not they knew Barrett from an earlier life but their association with him in Bennett turned them into miner miners quickly enough.

When the ice finally went out on May 28, 1898, almost 7,000 boats were launched into Bennett Lake during the summer months and the stampeders started on the final stage of their journey to the Klondike Gold Fields.

Barrett, Turner, and Geiger were not among their number. They remained in Bennett and formed a company – Turner and Co. – converting Barrett's tent from a liquor outlet into the Yukon Hotel.

Exactly why they stayed who can say for sure. Most miners of the miners were more opportunistic, moving on with the stampeders, plying their trade – whatever it may be – to extract as much money from them in as short a time as possible, and all the while waiting for the next gold strike to come along so they could move along to a fresh crop of naïve marks or desperately dry customers.

Barrett, Turner, and Geiger possibly believed they could make a go of it by remaining in Bennett and building a hotel that provided a higher

Bar in the new Yukon Hotel 1899

level of comfort and service rather than pursuing the miners to the gold fields. There was good reason to believe that.

Bennett had an air of permanence in 1898.

In February of that year the BC government made a town site grant to the owner of the Klondyke Hotel, Big Bill Anderson, to survey and divide the area into town lots for sale – a job which was completed in June. When the stampeders moved on in May, many stayed behind – apparently wanting to make Bennett their home. There were numerous businesses including a police station, a post office, two banks, and a newspaper.

The stampeders kept coming over the Chilkoot Trail. A number of companies were operating and building more steamers to travel between Bennett, as the head of navigation for the Yukon River, to Dawson City in the Klondike. A telegraph line was being planned from the coast. There was news that a railroad was going to be built from Skagway, Alaska, through the White Pass to Bennett.

In June, 1899, the Yukon Hotel moved from the tent beside the Dawson Hotel and down the street a short distance into a two-story building that – rather than having one room with 25 occupants – had 25 luxurious rooms, which could hold one or two occupants each.

There were gas lamps in the lobby, the bar, and every room. Thomas Geiger did the plumbing, which featured baths and toilets that drained directly into the lake behind the hotel. The exterior walls were covered with corrugated iron sheathing imported from Montreal, Quebec. The fixtures and fittings came from Victoria, BC. The hotel became one of the finest in the town with its large bar where players could be found crowded around several card tables and a piano upon which a tickler of the ivories performed each evening.

A month later the railroad arrived. In its wake more hotels and restaurants were built to accommodate travellers as they changed from the train to the steamships, and vice versa, to the point where Charles Maus Taylor wrote in his 1901 book Touring Alaska and the Yellowstone, "The town seems to consist almost entirely of saloons, restaurants and hotels.... It appears as though the people here do nothing but eat and sleep."

The competition got cutthroat. Many, but not all, of the restaurants, saloons, and hotels employed every gimmick they could to lure in the weary traveller – often including the hiring of prostitutes to hang around outside the establishment and entice customers to accompany them inside to indulge in whatever pleasures awaited them.

A Yukon Sun newspaper review in April, 1900, said of the Arctic Restaurant and Hotel operated by Fred Trump and Ernest Levin, "I would advise respectable women travelling alone, or with an escort, to be careful in their selection of hotels at Bennett.... For single men the Arctic has excellent accommodation as well as the best restaurant in Bennett, but I would not advise respectable women to go there to sleep as they are liable to hear that which would be repugnant to their feelings and uttered, too, by the depraved of their own sex."

However, Barrett and Turner must have seen the writing on the wall. Bennett was booming in 1899, with what seemed like a permanent population approaching 2,000 persons, but the end was near. The railroad was inevitably going to reach further inland, past Bennett into the Yukon to Caribou Crossing and Whitehorse. The head of navigation on the Yukon River was going to move with it. Unless the railroad decided to base their maintenance camp in Bennett the community would soon have no reason to exist – and there were suggestions that Caribou Crossing, 40 kilometres away at the north end of Bennett Lake, would be the preferred location.

In 1900, Barrett and Turner were in Whitehorse building the Grand Hotel on the corner of Main Street and Front Street – starting construction shortly before the final spike in the railroad was driven at Caribou Crossing on July 19, 1900, sealing Bennett's fate.

In 1901, Barrett and Turner sold the Grand Hotel and the two men seem to have left the north.

Geiger was never part of the Grand Hotel. He apparently remained in Bennett even as the community disintegrated but possibly also left the north in 1901.

The White Pass and Yukon Route (WPYR) railway confirmed Caribou Crossing as their maintenance station in 1900.

Many of the businesses in Bennett simply closed their doors, selling off their furniture and fixtures at bargain basement prices. Buildings were loaded on barges and floated to other communities or mining camps along the southern lakes of the Yukon. The Vendome Hotel was abandoned, sold, and eventually pulled across the ice of Bennett Lake in the winter of 1910-11, ending up in Caribou Crossing where it became part of the Matthew Watson General Store. King's Saw Mill was dismantled and shipped to Caribou Crossing where it continued operating for a few more years making rail ties for the railroad.

The WPYR bought some crumbling buildings located on the railway right-of-way and then demolished them because they posed a danger to train passengers wandering through the former town site. Other structures not located on railway land were abandoned, left to be consumed by the wilderness and/or stripped bare by scavengers. Today, the Gold Rush town's sole remaining original building is St. Andrew's Presbyterian Church, which was dedicated on May 24, 1899, and is maintained by Parks Canada's as a Recognized Federal Heritage Building.

By 1901, Bennett was almost a ghost town with less than 50 residents left – and they were packing up to leave. The Yukon Hotel, still resplendent with its fixtures and plumbing, was sold to William "Big Bill" Anderson but he had no intention of keeping it in Bennett. In May, 1901, Big Bill – who was also the owner of the now abandoned Klondyke Hotel in Bennett – loaded the Yukon Hotel on a scow and dragged it across the melting late spring ice of Lake Bennett to Caribou Crossing. There he deposited the structure on an empty lot opposite the train depot and renamed it the Anderson hotel.

Anderson's application for a hotel license in Caribou Crossing has caused some confusion over the years for historical researchers. It was written on Vendome Hotel stationary because he had also purchased that establishment at the same time he acquired the Yukon Hotel. Both buildings eventually ended up in Carcross and were located next door to each other. However, it was the metal cladding on the Yukon Hotel that gave the building its distinctive mark and still does on the surviving part of the original Caribou Hotel today.

Chapter 3

TODEZZANE

The Tagish people must have been shocked when George Holt appeared in their camps in the sand hills above Bennett Lake in 1874.

They may have heard of them but most probably hadn't ever actually seen a white man before. Others may have run across them while trading with the Tlingit people on the coast or with the Southern Tutchone and Athapaskans in the interior of what eventually became the Yukon Territory.

The north end of one of their mountain pass trading routes was the last place they expected to find a European.

When Europeans first turned up on the coast in the mid-1700s seeking furs the Tlingit determined they had to protect their traditional trading routes to the interior. They concealed the best mountain passes from the Russians and British, maintaining that secrecy even past the purchase of Alaska from Russia by the United States in 1867.

In the interior of the Yukon the Tlingits had already burned a Hudson's Bay Company trading post at Fort Selkirk in 1851 to curtail the European incursion from the east.

Chilkoot Jack, also known as Atlin Jack, believed to have guided the first white man across the Chilkoot Trail in 1874

It took the lure of gold bringing more people north to break the Tlingit trade monopoly. In 1873, gold prospectors were becoming increasingly more common in the Yukon River watershed but they had all arrived either by crossing the mountains in the eastern Yukon, overland from the south or via Norton Sound in western Alaska and all the way up the Yukon River. Holt – looking for another shorter avenue to the rumoured

Bennett townsite, 1898

gold fields of the Yukon – somehow managed to evade the men guarding the pass through the coastal mountains, apparently with the aid of a Tlingit guide, and became the first non-Indigenous person to reach the headwaters of the Yukon River by walking from the sea.

The Tlingits, realizing the inevitability of losing control over the mountain routes saw an opportunity and took full advantage of it. They had three major trading routes through the mountains – the Chilkat Pass, the Taku River, and the Chilkoot Trail – and directed the increasing number of gold seekers to their least important trading route over the Chilkoot while continuing to conceal the others.

They were upset when the American and Canadian governments told them they couldn't charge a toll to the stampeders streaming over their trail. They knew the US charged a toll for the use of government docks at Dyea and didn't understand why they couldn't do the same for the use of their land.

Blocked from collecting a tariff they advertised their skills as experienced mountain travellers and provided a service packing gear

Stone cribbing on Chilkoot Trail, 1979

over the pass. Each stampeder had to bring two tons of supplies over the mountains and they could either spend a month moving their outfit or hire packers to move it for them.

The Tagish people occupied the area around Bennett and Caribou Crossing for dozens of generations before Europeans made an appearance. Archaeological findings have proven there were people here even before the Tagish, although there is nothing to tell us what fate befell the Microblade people who left behind miniature stone and bone weapons used for killing prehistoric bison approximately 4,500 years ago.

The trade between the inland people and the coastal people had been going on long enough that the two peoples had generations earlier intermarried and merged many aspects of their cultures. Several of the

Tagish people joined the Tlingits in offering packing services over the mountains.

Inland Tlingit and Tagish Elders tell stories of life lived with the land where people followed an annual cycle, moving from camp to camp with each one having its own purpose. This one for picking berries. This one for fishing. This one for trapping. This one for hunting.

The land at the south end of Bennett Lake had plenty of blueberries, mossberries, lowbush cranberries, and other berries that were picked in the late summer and early fall. The lakes, streams, and rivers provided Inconnu, Trout, Whitefish, Burbot, and Herring year round. Furs for trading were collected off the trap lines through the latter part of the winter. Goats were hunted in the mountains south of Bennett Lake. Moose were plentiful just about anywhere.

Twice a year a Caribou herd crossed the narrows near the north end of Bennett Lake so the people would move there to harvest them and to fish. The narrows, which is, in reality, a short river with a substantial current, connected Bennett Lake to what the white prospectors initially called Tako Lake.

The Tagish people called the river Todezzane, "blowing all the time" – a reference to the seemingly never ceasing wind that blew off Bennett Lake. The Tlingit name was Naataase Heen, "water running through the narrows." Todezzane was used as a seasonal fishing and hunting camp.

While most of the people lived in a larger, less transient village at Tagish, "fish trap", on a wide river that connected Tako Lake to another large lake, Takwadada, "where sand washes up on shore." Takwadada was renamed Marsh Lake in 1885 by US Army explorer Frederick Schwatka.

Eventually, Tako Lake became known as Tagish Lake. It had two parts – the dangerously blustery Windy Arm on the west side and the longer, slightly less breezy Taku Arm to the east.

When the Klondike Gold Rush arrived in 1897 and stampeders used the narrows as a rest stop on the way to the gold fields they called it Caribou Crossing. The Caribou Crossing name was officially adopted in 1899 when the town site was being surveyed for the railway.

The Indigenous people believed that every living thing contained its own spirit. That the denizens of the wilderness were beings that people could not possess, but something they were honour bound to take care of. To respect the plant, or fish or animal, was to acknowledge the Creator and form a powerful and constant connection to the land.

The area at the north end of Bennett Lake was a particularly spiritual place. It was where the Tagish people believed that all the world's animals came from.

Long ago, said the Tagish Elders, Game Mother was living in the mountains near Lake Bennett. One spring, when she was nearing the end of a pregnancy, her husband and brothers decided they wanted to go to the coast. Game Mother decided to remain where she was because it was too late for her to travel.

When her time came, the Moose came out first. Game Mother taught Moose how to eat willows. Caribou was born next and she instructed him on how to lose his antlers and live off the mosses that grow high in the mountains.

Then came Grizzly Bear — whom she told to have a long sleep each year to conserve his great strength. Wolf, a lone and baneful predator. Beaver, with his industrious teeth and his beautiful fur coat that made him so important to the trapper. And all the other animals, whom she showed what to eat, how to live, and how to behave.

When she had taught them everything they needed to know and it was time for them to move across the land and look after themselves, Game Mother made a giant hammock and tied one corner of it to each mountain around Todezzane — Tekade'uch (Gopher Mountain, later renamed Montana Mountain), Weji'tsay (Grey Mountain), Cheli'chele (Caribou Mountain), and Tatlachechi (Nares Mountain). The animals all gathered on the hammock and had a great celebration where they danced and sang to each other. Then they bid farewell to one another and spread out across the land where they still live today.

Life wasn't easy for the people who lived with the land but it contented them. The arrival of thousands of Europeans on the way to the Klondike Gold Fields disrupted their lifestyle forever.

To build the boats and buildings in Bennett all the trees at the south end of Bennett Lake were cut down. The denuded landscape and massive volumes of traffic effectively wiped out the berries the Tagish

Sawblade and hiker on Chilkoot Trail

people collected. The amount of food needed to feed the hordes of stampeders put extreme stress on the fish populations, the goats in the mountains, and the moose. Being so easy to kill and so close to the tent town at Caribou Crossing, the Woodland Caribou were depleted almost to the point of extinction.

Tagish chief Skookum Jim, one of the co-discoverers of the Klondike gold, understood that although some of the changes to the countryside

Church steeple at Bennett

and to their lifestyle would be temporary — much of it was going to change them forever. When the WPYR started work near Caribou Crossing in 1898 he negotiated a deal with the company to provide jobs for his people in exchange for permission for the railroad to cross their traditional lands.

It was an agreement that still endured in 2018.

Because the railway maintenance camp was to be located in Caribou Crossing it spelled an end to the nomadic existence of the Tagish people and to the village at Tagish. While most still went trapping in the winter and fishing and hunting in the fall, having a job with the railway meant they had to live all or most of the year in Caribou Crossing.

The end of the Klondike Gold Rush and the abandoning of Bennett meant the trees and berries would eventually grow back. Fish, moose, and goat populations rebounded, but they were no longer essential to the survival of the people who now found subsistence in the goods for sale in the trading posts. The Woodland Caribou herd began to recover but they were still few in number.

The survey of Caribou Crossing in 1899 by the WPYR set aside a site for the Indigenous people to occupy on the south side of the narrows with the downtown core, government offices, and non-Indigenous population on the north side. When the people moved from their village at Tagish they went to the south shore of the narrows because, being on the lee side of Gopher Mountain, it provided better shelter from the bitter wind that constantly pummelled the north shore. Some chose to live on the north side because that was where they had camped before the white man arrived and the wind kept the mosquitoes down in the summer.

Caribou Crossing became the main railhead for construction of the WPYR's northern section from Bennett, BC, to Whitehorse, Yukon. It was the first permanent community in the north to be established based solely upon its importance to transportation in the region.

In 1901, Anglican Bishop William Bompas arrived in Caribou Crossing to establish a mission school for Indian children. After 40 years of mission work in the north, he wrote in his journal that Caribou Crossing was chosen as the location for his school because it "forms the centre of a hitherto un-occupied area, and forges perhaps one of the last links of the chains of Christian Missionary Society Stations which girded the world."

He brought children from communities along the entire length of the Yukon River to his school in a well-intentioned, but ill-conceived venture to separate them from family and tradition and provide them "an ordinary school education...the things most necessary to lift them to something nearer to the Christian standard of cleanliness and industry...and numberless other things that will be useful in the kind of life they will lead."

Irked by inconsistent mail delivery he petitioned the Canadian government in 1903 to change the name from Caribou Crossing to the abbreviated "Carcross" to avoid confusion with other northern communities also called Caribou Crossing. The post office approved the change in 1904.

The bishop also decreed that Indigenous people should stay on one side of the river and white people on the other. Most of the Tagish people who had initially chosen to stay on the north side of the narrows moved to the south side. The community, which had not been divided prior to the decree, was divided after it.

Chapter 4

BIG BILL ANDERSON

"Big Bill" Anderson either arrived in the north with a lot of money or the Klondyke Hotel in Bennett did boom-time business during its short working life in Bennett. Possibly he made his fortune from the government contract to survey the Bennett town site in 1898.

However he earned his money, after the expense of purchasing two hotels in Bennett then moving one of them to Caribou Crossing in May, 1901, he realized the town wasn't yet big enough to support two hotels. There was another William – William Walmsley – who had just purchased a local roadhouse in anticipation of turning it into a first-class hotel. Walmsley had apparently been involved with the hotel business in Bennett, although it's not clear which establishment he was associated with.

Big Bill immediately either sold or walked away from the Vendome Hotel in Bennett and put the Anderson Hotel up for sale in November. There was no immediate interest from prospective buyers so he started establishing his hotel as the social and hospitality centre of the growing town before his pending competitor could open.

Hotels were either floated or pulled over the ice from Bennett to other communities. The Vendome Hotel and the Yukon Hotel were both moved in this manner to Carcross

He opened a small store in the hotel to attract a clientele different from the usual hotel bar flies and advertised that the Anderson Hotel was "a first class hotel" with a "bath house in connection" and served "only the best of liquors and cigars." The hotel sponsored community events, one of them being a Turkey Shoot in late December, 1901.

"Caribou can boast of more crack shots than any other town of its size in Canada," bragged the Whitehorse Star on Dec. 27, 1901, "and the entire population turned out to take part and witness the contest. A noticeable feature was the entire absence of drunkenness, not a single intoxicated person being present. The Indians took an active part in the proceedings, and every turkey was hotly contested for. Paddie, of Tagish, carried off the honors for the day."

"Big Bill" pursued the idea of buying out his competition then Walmsley stopped operating Caribou House in 1901. Anderson may actually have purchased it from him as he suggested in a letter to the mining recorder in Whitehorse in July, 1902. The correspondence also indicated that although Walmsley might no longer be in the hotel business he was still a nuisance.

Anderson Hotel letterhead

"I have heard that Scott Bros. are negotiating with William Walmsley for the sale of their building which he intends turning into a hotel," he wrote. "Now I have invested a great sum of money, in fact all I had, fixing up my house and buying Walmsley out and as times are so dull there is not any chance of getting it back. Instead it pinches me to keep, even having to keep, a cook when there is no person to eat. The bar business here is very light and there is not trade enough to one hotel besides two and if he starts a hotel it won't be worth living."

Lakeview and Wynton Hotels at Wynton waiting for customers

Wynton graveyard in 2016

All the while he kept advertising the hotel as being for sale. "For Sale (cheap)," read his ad in the Whitehorse Star in November 1901, "Finely furnished hotel with all the latest improvements, bath etc." In 1902, an interested buyer turned up.

"I am going out for a month or so," he wrote to the Gold Commissioner in Whitehorse on Dec. 30. "I sold out my hotel and store. That is if the man don't go back on his word."

On Feb. 25, 1903, the Anderson Hotel was sold to "Dawson Charlie (an Indian)" for a rumoured $9,000, although the bill of sale indicated that title was transferred for a mere one dollar.

While he was no longer the owner of the hotel in Caribou Crossing Big Bill was by no means finished with the hotel business. He operated two establishments in Discovery, in the gold fields near Atlin, BC in 1903-04, then two more in Dawson City in 1905.

With the gold seekers chasing their dreams further west into Alaska and business in the Klondike starting to flag, Big Bill returned to the southern Yukon and built one final hotel – the Lakeview – at Wynton, a spot on the map located at the south end of Tagish Lake's Windy Arm.

The plan was to provide a place of leisure for miners working in the burgeoning Big Thing Mine and living in Conrad City, located midway on Tagish Lake between Wynton and Caribou Crossing. He wasn't the only one with that idea. Another hotelier, Alex McDonald, built the Wynton

Hotel right next door to the Lakeview at the same time. Alex also owned a hotel in Conrad City – the Yukon Hotel.

If Big Bill thought that business was slow in Caribou Crossing in 1902, he hadn't seen anything yet.

Building lodgings at Wynton was purely speculative but there were early indicators that such a venture might actually work. In early 1905, the WPYR surveyed a possible spur line along Windy Arm to service the mines being developed along it before announcing an indefinite delay in the project until there was "sufficient business in sight to make a railroad to the mines profitable."

Some of the WPYR surveyors and workers had camped in the Wynton area. There was talk of a road from Conrad to Wynton. A route was surveyed and work started on its construction but that idea too was abandoned. There was faint hope when the steamship Gleaner and the barge Taku were wintered at Wynton that year but when launched again in the spring of 1906, they never returned.

Without any transportation connection to Wynton the 300 or more people living in Conrad City in 1906 weren't inclined to go to there for a room, meal or drink and there was no alternative source of potential customers.

Many Carcross old-timers tell an apocryphal tale of Alex and Big Bill in which one of them would go to the other hotel, slap a coin on the bar and order a drink. When he was finished imbibing the two would walk over to the other hotel where the second man would slap the same coin on the bar and order a drink. Then they would repeat the same routine as often as they could each day. It was apparently the only business that either place had in any given day. The two men became fast friends and the poor coin was eventually worn so badly it was barely recognizable.

Shortly after completing construction of their respective hotels in May, 1906, Alex McDonald sold the Wynton and Big Bill Anderson appears to have departed the north after selling the Lakeview the following year.

There is nothing left to identify where the hotels stood although ruins of smaller structures and three graves – two still occupied and one empty (the body was exhumed and repatriated) – can still be found.

Chapter 5

THE IMPORTANCE OF CARIBOU

The Tagish and Inland Tlingit people hunted most of the animals in the mountains around Todezzane. Each animal provided something different. If you needed meat it was the moose that could provide the most. For lightweight clothes, trade goods, and portable accommodations, it was the hide of the woodland caribou they prized above all else.

In their traditional stories about long-ago time when people and animals could still talk to one another the caribou are the animals most frequently mentioned. More recent stories speak of them as a person's medicine or power.

According to histories passed down through generations the caribou had at one time been so numerous that when herds crossed the side of a mountain it seemed the land itself was moving. The people followed predictable paths of migrating caribou each spring and fall. They built camps near where the herds travelled and constructed rock "blinds" behind which they hid until the animals came close enough to be hit with a spear, dart or arrow.

Nothing went to waste. The meat was dried and eaten. The hide was easy to work with – thin and light, but warm and tough for clothing,

Caribou swimming Yukon River c1930

blankets, and moccasins. Sinew was flexible and durable, valued for sewing. Antlers were carved into awls for cleaning the flesh off fresh hides. Bones, unusually strong for their size, turned into arrowheads, construction material, and tools. Hoofs weighed down fishing nets, decorated blankets, and turned into children's toys.

Trade was important between the people of the southern Yukon and the coastal peoples from Alaska. Caribou hide clothes were particularly desired by the coastal people.

Caribou populations started to decline approximately 1,200 years ago when a volcanic explosion, on what is now known as Mount Churchill, in the extreme southwest corner of Alaska, smothered the southern Yukon with a thick layer of ash. The ash devastated the plant life, which in turn meant that grazing animals like moose, bison, and caribou starved.

Most of the people who inhabited the region at that time may have left, moving south through what is now the province of Alberta where some remained. It is believed by some anthropologists that others probably traveled as far south to what is today the state of Arizona.

In geological time the ash was a mere blip. Within a couple of generations fresh foliage eventually emerged from below the ash and over the next 400 years animals, including a genetically different caribou that is today called the Woodland Caribou, gradually returned.

The food the caribou depended upon had changed somewhat and the vast herds that once thrived on the mountains continued to diminish even as the number of people dependent upon them increased. The weapons used by the Indigenous people became more efficient during this time as they switched from the atlatl and dart to the more accurate and deadly bow and arrow.

When Europeans arrived they came with rifles and were able to harvest caribou in ever increasing numbers.

Caribou were still plentiful as recently as the 1930s but continuing human encroachment on their feeding and breeding grounds combined with ongoing climate change affected the tree lichens and ground cover

upon which their survival depended. In 1993, the Carcross/Tagish First Nation proposed a hunting ban for both Indigenous and Non-Indigenous hunters to enable the herd, which had been reduced to approximately 350 animals, to recover. Northern Woodland Caribou were listed and protected in 2005 as endangered under Canada's federal Species At Risk Act. Since then their numbers have increased slightly.

Even though they were no longer a subsistence food caribou remained central to the Tagish and Tlingit cultures. When the construction of a resort was proposed close to Carcross at Milhaven Bay in 2014 with its promises of employment and prosperity, it was the environment and its effect on caribou that created concern among the people of the Carcross/Tagish First Nation.

At first, elder Edna Helm didn't think the resort was a bad idea but after pondering on the plan for a while she changed her mind.

"Since then I have grown to appreciate what I've got and stuff that's around here and I've learned since then about our caribou loss, our moose loss, our fish are declining, all these things have been happening and I've grown to find out," she said in an interview with the Yukon News. "All this stuff is going to have an impact on the environment here; that's what I'm worried about.

"I haven't shot a caribou in...gosh...20 years or so because we're trying to bring them back and then they're going to put a resort up there with all that stuff in our caribou country?"

Chapter 6

DAWSON CHARLIE

An amendment to the Canadian Government's Indian Act in 1884 made it a felony for "Indians" to purchase alcohol, consume alcohol or to even enter a licensed establishment. The act had already made it a crime to sell alcohol not only to "Indians", but to anyone "...who follows the Indian mode of life, or any child of such person...."

While the act had effectively criminalized both the seller and buyer of liquor, it had a number of loopholes in it. It didn't address the issue of Indigenous people possessing alcohol (which they didn't buy and weren't consuming), selling alcohol to Non-Indigenous people or owning a bar – possibly because the law makers couldn't imagine a situation where an "Indian" could afford to own one or they believed the amendment stopping them from entering a bar would suffice.

Dawson Charlie (Tagish name: Káa Goox) was known as Tagish Charlie in his younger days when he worked as a packer for prospectors crossing the coastal mountains from Dyea, Alaska. He and his uncle, Skookum Jim (Keish), earned a reputation for being reliable, truthful, and competent while working for William Ogilvie. Ogilvie was the Canadian government's

Dawson Charlie (Káa Goox)

Dominion Land Surveyor from 1887-89 and hired them to assist with his survey of the Chilkoot Pass and the US-Canada boundary.

He changed his name to Dawson Charlie after the Klondike Gold Rush turned Dawson City into the largest city in North America west of Winnipeg and north of San Francisco and to recognize his role in the discovery. Also because there was another man named Tagish Charlie, from a different clan, already living at Todezzane.

Dawson Charlie's younger sibling, Patsy Henderson (Koolseen), who was with Charlie when gold was discovered, claimed his older brother was the first to find gold in the Klondike Valley.

"Dawson Charlie find ten cent nugget," Patsy told tens of thousands of tourists over three decades of storytelling in Carcross, "He didn't find in creek. Find on hillside on slide on top of rock."

Patsy accompanied his brother and Skookum Jim from Todezzane in early 1896, when they set out to find George Carmacks and his wife Kate (Shaaw Tláa) – Skookum Jim's sister – who had travelled north down the Yukon River two years earlier.

Skookum Jim, Patsy maintained, was the one who had discovered gold in Rabbit Creek, later renamed Bonanza Creek, and sparked the worldwide frenzy that was the Klondike Gold Rush. Patsy's assertion was backed up by government surveyor William Ogilvie, who became the Commissioner of the Yukon Territory from 1898-1901. George Carmack was officially declared the discoverer of gold because he was a white man and they didn't believe the government officials would accept an Indigenous person in that role.

Regardless of who discovered the gold, the Klondike Valley made the three men – George Carmack, Dawson Charlie, and Skookum Jim – wealthy and famous.

After a few years of working their gold claims the three traveled south to Seattle, Washington, and San Francisco, California, to celebrate their good fortune. Dawson Charlie soon got bored with visiting the big cities and entertained himself by throwing handfuls of fifty-cent pieces out the window of his hotel room and watching the people below scramble around chasing the bouncing coins. He stopped only when the police threatened to arrest him for creating a traffic hazard.

(Front row L to R) Dawson Charlie (third from left),Kate Carmack, Graphie Carmack (seated), George Carmack, Skookum Jim Mason and Patsy Henderson on the S.S. Roanoke, bound for San Francisco

Both he and Skookum Jim struggled with life outside the Yukon. They missed living off the land – hunting moose, picking berries, prospecting, and fishing. Both men longed for the days where they could climb to the tops of hills and gaze out over the splendour of the unspoiled wilderness or savour the simple pleasure of drinking teeth-numbing cold water from a mountain stream.

Their discomfort resulted in both men being arrested and fined for public intoxication in Seattle along with Kate Carmack in July, 1899. Then their partnership with George Carmack fell apart in August, 1900. A year later they returned home, along with Kate Carmack, to what was now known as Caribou Crossing.

Dawson Charlie apparently wasn't a heavy drinker, although he could afford to be. A report prepared by the Skookum Jim Friendship Centre in

March, 1992, suggested that he didn't drink all the time but when he did his "thirst was extravagant".

Because of the law, if an "Indian" wanted a drink, he or she had to buy their alcohol from a bootlegger, find a place of concealment where the police couldn't see them, and drink it down as quickly as possible.

Rather than trying to get alcohol surreptitiously and drinking it on the sly, Dawson Charlie decided to take advantage of the loopholes in the Indian Act by purchasing the Anderson Hotel, remodelling it, and renaming it the Caribou Hotel – thereafter simply called "the Caribou".

Because he wasn't allowed to enter the bar in his new acquisition or purchase the liquor inventory, he hired a white man, Mr. Scott, to manage it for him. Over the next few years, the managers of the Caribou possibly had problems working for an "Indian" or maybe Dawson Charlie was just difficult to work for. Mr. Scott was gone before the end of 1903, replaced briefly by Theodore Watson, then by Mrs. E. Ready in 1904, who, in turn, was replaced by R.J. Brittan in 1906.

Other than owning the hotel Dawson Charlie had no interest in the business and spent his time out on the land with Skookum Jim prospecting for gold. On July 4, 1903, he staked the discovery claim on Fourth of July Creek near Kluane Lake – a massive body of water almost 300 kilometres northwest of Caribou Crossing and ignited a second, much smaller gold rush.

Earlier in the summer he registered another discovery claim on what eventually became Dawson Charlie Creek – a tributary to the Wheaton River, which emptied into Bennett Lake just a few kilometres from Caribou Crossing. It wouldn't be until 1906 that a short-lived stampede attracted about 600 prospectors to the Watson River within hailing distance of Dawson Charlie's claim in the Wheaton River Valley.

Being a hotel owner was likely a factor in his application for Canadian citizenship in 1904 in addition to his fame as the co-discoverer of gold in the Klondike. At the time Indigenous people were not considered citizens of Canada. Under the Indian Act, in addition to not being able to purchase or drink liquor, they couldn't vote, sue or be sued, be called for jury duty or hold any type of public office. There were extremely rare exceptions but each exemption had to be individually granted by a special act of the Canadian parliament.

Caribou Hotel in Caribou Crossing, c1903-1906

On July 2, 1904, Dawson Charlie, who applied under his "legal" name of Charley Henderson, became the first Indigenous person in the Yukon to be exempted from the Indian Act and proclaimed to have "all the rights and privileges of a white citizen" because he was a "man of considerable means" who did not "follow the Indian mode of life" and was "intelligent, capable, temperate in habits, and a good citizen."

Business was so good in 1905 that the Scott and Caribou Hotels joined together to throw a free Christmas party for all the single men in the Tagish Lake-Bennett Lake-Carcross area. Two fiddlers and a pianist accompanied the men and a few women from Carcross as they danced into the wee hours of the next morning.

It wasn't all positive news for Dawson Charlie. Along with his wealth and Canadian citizenship came the stress of balancing his traditional lifestyle with the materialism of his moneyed Non-native status – something he was never able to accomplish just as he hadn't been able to adapt to the big city culture.

It affected his marriage, resulting in a separation from his wife Annie (Sadusge) in 1905, making him a single father to a three-year-old son and five-year old daughter at a time when single parents were frowned upon by Victorian society. According to the Whitehorse Star, he was arrested and fined for being intoxicated three or four times in 1906.

The missteps in his personal life eventually cost him his exemption from the Indian Act. According to the Whitehorse Star on Jan. 1, 1909, he was "returned to his pristine condition" just before Christmas, 1906 although the Caribou, since it continued being managed by a white man, was still able to operate its bar.

Business was brisk at the Caribou in 1906. All the customers Big Bill Anderson had been waiting for in Wynton were to be found in Carcross.

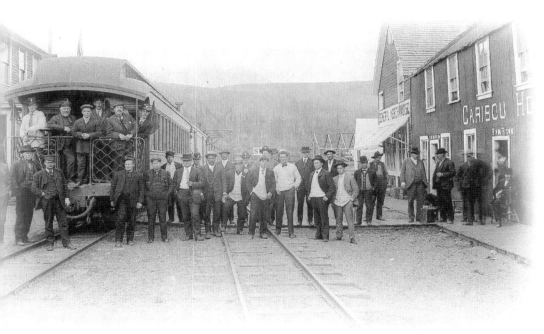

Downtown Carcross, 1903. There is a woman leaving the main door of the Caribou Hotel bar, which was unusual since women had to use their own entrance at the time.

Skookum Jim Mason (Keish)

Chapter 7

THE LEGENDS HOLD COURT

Government officials. Railroad men. Mine investors and speculators. Tourists. Miners. Trappers. Dreamers and achievers. Professional gamblers garbed in their con man best and woodcutters from King's Sawmill, sawdust coated and sweaty. The filthy rich and the unwashed destitute. All of them were rubbing shoulders with each other in Carcross in 1906.

Because the WPYR was the only rail link to anywhere, almost everything and everyone who came into or left the Yukon and central Alaska had to pass through Carcross. Even after US President Warren Harding drove the golden spike to complete the Alaska Railroad, connecting Alaska's interior to the coast in 1923, it was still more convenient and less expensive for people living along the Yukon River to go "outside" via Carcross and Skagway.

While Whitehorse was the northern terminus of the railroad and the southern head of navigation for riverboat traffic on the Yukon River, Carcross was the control point where the riverboat traffic on the southern lakes connected with the train tracks and hosted the main rail yard for maintaining both the tracks and the trains that travelled on them.

The Caribou wasn't the only hotel in town. John and Alfred Scott – the same Scott brothers who had been dickering with William Walmsley to sell him a building to use as a hotel – had gotten into the business for themselves. Walmsley had decided not to purchase the building from the Scotts, instead buying another hotel, Caribou House, from Charles Zorn in 1901. The Scott brothers then bought that establishment from Walmsley in 1903, renamed it Hotel Scott, and billed it as the "Only First Class Hotel in Carcross...headquarters for mining men and travelers."

Competition to rent rooms was fierce but lucrative for all – despite the fact that the stench of stale tobacco smoke, skunky beer, and whiskey wafted through the hallways and permeated the accommodations in both hotels. However, when it came to the café and bar trade the Caribou had two advantages the others didn't – Dawson Charlie and Skookum Jim.

Skookum Jim was a regular at the Caribou because Dawson Charlie owned it and everyone wanted to eat and drink with two of the men who discovered Klondike Gold. Both spun fanciful tales of packing for prospectors over the Chilkoot Trail, fishing at the mouth of the Klondike River, discovering the nuggets in Rabbit Creek that led to the Klondike Gold Rush, their adventures in Seattle and San Francisco, and their discovery of gold in both the Kluane Lake region and near the Wheaton River, sparking smaller gold rushes.

"Gold is where you find it" is the old adage that governs prospecting and Skookum Jim possessed a knack for finding it. Dawson Charlie had an innate ability to figure out how best to get it out of the ground.

They talked of future prospecting ventures, with their audience hanging on every word because they might let slip that one clue that tipped their hand as to where the two were thinking about heading next – and that sliver of information might determine whether the listener could become a future king of the gold fields as well.

Even though the Klondike Gold Rush was over and the bulk of the stampeders had headed into Alaska in pursuit of gold finds near Fairbanks, Iditarod, Nome, and numerous other places, the gold creeks of the Klondike were still productive. Mining records during the first decade of the 20th century ranked the area as the world's fourth largest gold producer.

Outside of the Klondike itself the largest concentration of miners and mining corporations in Canada's Northwest was on the lakes around Carcross.

Among the throng in the Caribou would have been "Colonel" John Conrad – he was an oversized man with an even bigger ego, had a healthy appetite for cigars and whiskey, and embodied the risk-taker philosophy that if you're not standing on the edge, you're taking up too much room. Artist Emily Carr described him as "mammoth" and sketched a picture of him in her personal journal as he "compressed" her between himself and the train window when they met while riding the White Pass railroad in 1907.

Although it was a rank that stuck with him after his time in the north, John Conrad wasn't actually a Colonel. That tongue-in-cheek title had been granted to him in 1905 by a news reporter after he bragged about how he singlehandedly saved Canada's entire north from economic disaster with his mining venture on Windy Arm.

John was a scion of a wealthy Montana ranching family that had inherited a great deal of money after an 1889 battle over a large estate was settled when the primary beneficiary – the colonel's grandmother on his mother's side – drank from a bottle she received as a gift. It was labelled as whiskey but turned out to be coloured water laced with arsenic and it was never determined who gave it to her.

He had been involved in an acrimonious divorce from a prominent East Coast socialite where every ugly, sordid detail and accusation ended up on the front page of the Helena Independent – the largest newspaper in Montana's capital city.

The colonel was the owner of the Big Thing Mine and had a small town, Conrad City (the same Conrad City upon which Big Bill Anderson had staked his Wynton gamble) along with an aerial tramline that ran 11 kilometres across the face of Gopher Mountain – which he decided should be called Montana Mountain.

In the summer months, the ore from his mine was carried up Windy Arm twice a week to the docks at Carcross by the steamship Gleaner, loaded on the train, and taken to the coast. In 1905, a rough 18-kilometre wagon road was built along with a new telegraph line between Conrad and Carcross. The new wagon road included a bascule bridge, built across the narrows at Carcross. Its centre section could be raised like a drawbridge to make way for steamships traveling between Bennett and Tagish Lakes. The railroad bridge had been constructed with a turntable apparatus that spun the central section sideways to allow the ships passage.

With an all-season land link and twice-weekly summer trips by the Gleaner, Conrad, his employees, business partners, and investors spent time in the Caribou listening to Dawson Charlie and Skookum Jim. Conrad himself didn't need to rent a room. He owned a large house just around the corner from the hotel.

Another regular in the audience was Captain James Alexander – a tall, powerfully built man whose rank came from his time in the British Army in South Africa during the Boer War.

James was an investor in, and manager of, the Engineer Gold Mine, simply called "Engineer" and located near the south end of Taku Arm. In 1906, he had ambitious plans for himself and the mine.

When he went about squeezing out his partners and other investors it was a hostile activity that allegedly involved blackmail, misrepresentation, and the improper filing of claims. One of the displaced partners – a Mr. Brown who, depending upon which account you read, was either a lawyer in Skagway, Alaska, or a businessman from Atlin, BC – placed a curse on all persons involved with the mine. "Nothing but death and disaster," he wrote in a letter in 1912, "will be the lot of anyone associated with Engineer Mine."

It was an invocation that may have ultimately claimed 17 lives, including James himself, and left the Caribou Hotel a legacy that would become world renowned.

James's "wife" Louise likely accompanied him. Diminutive and charming, she enjoyed a cigar and a good shot of whiskey as much as the next woman, revelled in the company of miners, and loved having them bend her ear with their tales. After their deaths there was no paperwork to verify she and the Captain ever married and another wife with a teenage daughter turned up from England to contest the will.

Like Conrad City, Engineer Mine relied on the Gleaner to ferry men, ore, and supplies back and forth to Carcross during the summer months. In winter, horses pulled heavily loaded sleds over the frozen lakes.

Colonel Conrad

Also mixed in with the crowd were Otto and Kate Partridge. The couple, who always dressed elegantly — he in his Prince Albert suit and she in long gowns with lace collars and a scarf wrapped fashionably around her neck — operated the Ben-My-Chree (Gaelic meaning "Girl of my Heart") Mine at the farthest southern tip of Taku Arm.

They didn't go to the Caribou just because they had a taste for cigars and whiskey. They went because they understood how society worked and why it was important to be seen in the right place at the right time. Hobnobbing with Skookum Jim and Dawson Charlie was as prestigious as it got in the Yukon.

Otto, who lived a privileged early life in England, climbed the Chilkoot Trail in 1897 seeking adventure more than gold. When he reached Bennett, rather than pressing on to the Klondike gold fields, he started a company building steamships for the southern lakes. Kate followed him over the Chilkoot a year later. They ran a sawmill at Milhaven Bay, a short distance up Bennett Lake from Carcross, manufacturing railway ties for the WPYR.

The two were well connected with the British aristocracy – they had numerous relatives sitting in the House of Lords and the number increased with each telling of the tale of just how well connected they were.

Otto and Kate could have left the Yukon and returned to being a part of the upper crust of English society but they weren't able to bring themselves to leave the little paradise they had found in one of the remotest regions of the North American continent.

Ben-My-Chree was unique in the world – an isolated microclimate that defied the northern winter and stretched out the summer. A haven for wildlife. A horticulturist's dream. Surrounded by tall snow-capped mountains and massive glaciers that reached from their back door through the coastal mountains to the Pacific Ocean. The only way to get there was on the Gleaner and the only way to get out was to go to Carcross.

It would take a disaster in 1911 for Otto and Kate to withdraw from the mining industry and unlock the true potential of their chosen home. It was a decision that would turn their remote estate into a holiday destination for the world's wealthy, powerful, and famous and make the Caribou a well-known hotel in the upper levels of society on both sides of the Atlantic Ocean.

The paddle wheeler Gleaner was a lifeline for the mines in the southern lakes. Not only did Engineer, Ben-My-Chree, and Conrad depend upon her, but she was a valuable link in connecting the gold fields at Atlin and Discovery with the "outside" (any place outside of the Yukon River watershed – which pretty much encompasses all of the Yukon and Alaska). It was not a simple decision nor an easy task to undertake the journey "outside."

The steamer Scotia carried ore, supplies, and passengers across Atlin Lake from the gold fields to the terminus of the Taku Tram – a three-kilometre railway connecting Atlin Lake and Taku Arm.

A miniature train engine, nicknamed "The Duchess", pulled them across the portage over what may have been the shortest set of railroad tracks

MR & MRS. O.H PARTRIDGE. BEN MY CHREE. B.C.

Otto and Kate Partridge at Ben-My-Chree

on earth at the time. The Duchess was underpowered and, on the uphill eastbound trips, the passengers would often be asked to climb off and help push the train. There was no turnaround at the east end of the railway so the train had to run in reverse to return to the west end.

At the eastern end of the railway they boarded the Gleaner to Carcross, spent the night, and hopped the train to Skagway before taking a coastal steamer to Vancouver or Seattle.

Coming from Dawson City would take the better part of a week to travel upstream on the Yukon River to catch the train to Skagway. From communities in central Alaska, a traveller usually had to add on another several days just to get to Dawson City. Going "outside" could take anywhere from two days to two weeks just to get to Carcross. From there you still had to get to Skagway and take a ship down the coast to reach the starting point for the journey that you actually wanted to take.

It is likely that the two major players in the Klondike River Valley gold dredging operations, Joe Boyle and Arthur Treadwell, would have both frequented the hotel on their numerous trips in and out of the Yukon on the WPYR. While the train was stopped to reload water and wood as well as unloading and loading freight and ore from the surrounding mine there was little else to do in Carcross except hang out with the two mining legends holding court in the Caribou or buy souvenirs at Elliott's Ivory shop just down the road.

Other one-time or occasional non-mining visitors would have included Frank Gotch (a wrestler who left the Yukon in 1903 and became world heavyweight champion and one of the most popular athletes in the United States in 1908), Alexander Pantages (who founded the Pantages Theatre chain in the United States with money earned as a saloon owner in Dawson City), "Klondike Kate" Rockwell (the woman Pantages jilted and who later sued him in a sensational and sordid trial that made the front page of major newspapers across North America), and the future middleweight boxing champion of the world, Jack "Twin" Sullivan – who liked Dawson City and returned periodically to the north to box local pugilists between 1900 and 1910.

Another was Robert Service, whose verse about the Yukon helped make him the most commercially successful poet of the 20th century, starting with his first book The Spell of the Yukon, which earned him a million dollars when published in 1907. He occasionally rode the train to Carcross when he had time off from his job as a banker in Whitehorse. It has been speculated by some historians that his poetry was inspired in part by the time he spent in the Caribou. The man who provided Service with the name for his most famous poetic character, Sam McGee, worked in the mines on Montana Mountain at the time.

With the exception of Service most non-mining visitors wouldn't have gone into the Caribou specifically to spend time with Skookum Jim and Dawson Charlie. It would have been to kill some time while taking the train out of the country and it always stopped for a long time in Carcross.

Like most winter nights the hotel bar and restaurant crowd was sparse the night of Friday, January 25, 1908.

It was late when the last customer finally left the Caribou. Skookum Jim had gone home hours before. Dawson Charlie headed over to the Scott Hotel in the early hours of Saturday morning, possibly for a final drink before walking over the railway bridge to his frame house on the south side of the narrows. There he got into an argument with another younger man who allegedly had a reputation for being violent when drinking. Then he left the hotel to walk home. Witnesses in the bar said he was drunk when he went out the door.

A short while later, a woman living on the top floor of the WPYR depot heard the sound of sleigh runners clacking across the railway ties on the train bridge. The sleigh stopped. She thought she heard the thud of something being dumped on the ice, then the sleigh moved on again, off the noisy bridge then silently away into the cold and dark.

A little more than a day after Dawson Charlie failed to turn up at his home his body was found and retrieved from the narrows by Skookum Jim and another friend. The official story was that he was inebriated and, while crossing the bridge, had stumbled and fallen to the ice below.

When the woman from the WPYR depot told her story barstool and café coffee detectives reached their own deduction. They were aware of the argument in the Scott Hotel, knew the reputation of the younger man, and determined that the timing of the sleigh coincided with the approximate time that Dawson Charlie would have been crossing the bridge. The only logical conclusion, they decided, was murder. Someone had pushed or thrown Dawson Charlie off that bridge.

No fresh snow had fallen that night so Dawson Charlie's footprints onto the bridge and any tracks possibly left by sled runners couldn't be distinguished from others who had crossed the bridge previously in the day. There was no conclusive evidence of foul play and the police ended the official investigation.

If it was murder it remains unsolved and the occasional subject of barstool sleuthing to this day.

Although the celebration of potlatches was outlawed under an 1884 amendment to the Indian Act, Skookum Jim was determined his nephew was going to get a traditional farewell from his people. It was a risky decision. To even encourage someone else to participate in a potlatch was a misdemeanour in Canadian law that could earn the offender two to six months in jail. The ban wasn't repealed until 1951.

Both the Tlingit and the Tagish people use the word "Potlatch" to describe celebrations of special occasions, especially the memorial ceremony held one or two years after an individual's death.

Dawson Charlie's Potlatch in Carcross, 1912

It is a gift-giving ritual where the deceased's family or clan demonstrate their wealth and prominence by distributing gifts to the guests attending the potlatch. The status of an individual or a family was established not by who kept the most possessions, but by who gave them away at a potlatch.

Dawson Charlie and Skookum Jim were both members of the Wolf clan. The other Tagish clan is the Crow and it fell to the Crow clan to be the hosts during the potlatch itself. During the event, which can last an indefinite amount of time, there is constant dancing, storytelling, and feasting.

After a generation of being banned there were not many people left who remembered the old ways of the Tagish. However, the few who did believed tradition requiring a potlatch outweighed the white man's law forbidding it.

The Wolf clan were determined to make Dawson Charlie's potlatch one that would be talked about for generations to come. It was held in November, 1912.

Skookum Jim and Patsy Henderson donated the cash to buy the food. Others scrounged up a few hundred trade blankets to distribute as gifts and the Crow clan prepared the village to host visitors who would be living there for an indeterminate period of time. People were invited from villages all across the southern Yukon. They came in droves. Men. Women. Children. Dogs. Some of them walking over 300 kilometres to get there.

As they approached Carcross they started firing their rifles into the air and continued shooting all the way through town and across the railway bridge Dawson Charlie fell or had been pushed from. It was, a then 14-year-old Johnnie Johns recalled, "Just like a war had begun."

The police exercised discretion and faded away, allowing the potlatch to proceed without any interference. Nor did the Crown ever prosecute the organizers.

When all who were coming had finally assembled they spent two weeks celebrating. Breakfast, lunch, and dinner were provided every day.

Matthew Watson, a white man who had recently purchased the general merchandise store next door to the Caribou Hotel, took photographs of the crowds, the feasting, and the dancing. How he talked himself into being allowed to attend isn't clear — white people were generally not invited at that time — but he later made postcards out of one of his images and sold them to tourists.

It became known as "The Last Big Potlatch" and almost 60 years passed before another of comparable impact was held.

Dawson Charlie's will named his wife Annie, from whom he had been separated for three years, as the primary beneficiary of his still fairly substantial estate.

Since separating from Dawson Charlie, Annie had met and married Arthur "Shorty" (a nickname he acquired because he was actually very tall) Auston, a member of the Northwest Mounted Police posted at Tagish. They lived and worked on a trapline/mink farm in the Wheaton River Valley near a small lake that was later named after her — Annie Lake — because Arthur was forced to resign from the Mounties after marrying an Indigenous woman.

According to her granddaughter Annie didn't know what to with the hotel. She had no interest in operating it and wanted to sell but Arthur suggested she hang onto it for the foreseeable future. On September 1, 1908, she entered into a lease-to-purchase agreement with Edwin and Bessie Gideon.

Chapter 8

WIPED OFF
THE FACE
OF THE
EARTH

Life in gold rush towns was harsh and unpredictable at the best of times coupled with the ever-present risk of man-made disaster at any time. The greatest nemesis of every boom-time community was fire.

Because towns were being constructed in a hurry most builders used the cheapest and most easily accessible materials available, which was wood salvaged from other buildings or fresh-cut logs. The only insulation available was the sawdust created by cutting the lumber so boxes were constructed around the lower part of the exterior wall, filled with the cuttings, and covered over. Newspapers were nailed to the walls inside the building to insulate the parts of the walls that didn't have the sawdust. There was little in the building that wouldn't burn well.

Makeshift heat traps were built around woodstove chimneys to make them more efficient at keeping temperatures tolerable in the poorly insulated structures. The heat traps also made them more prone to chimney fires, which, once started, were almost impossible to extinguish.

Chimney fires may have been the most frequent culprit, but definitely not the only one. Fire destroyed towns and cities from Chicago, Illinois, where Mrs. O'Leary's cow allegedly kicked over a lantern in 1871 to San Francisco in May, 1850, where arson was suspected but never proven.

Dawson City was torched twice – in 1897, when a dance hall girl threw a lantern at a rival and again the next year when a candle was left burning unattended – apparently by the same dance hall girl. Whitehorse's downtown was razed to the ground in 1905 when fire broke out in a barbershop.

Anne Morgan and Tutshi at back of Caribou Hotel, 2015. Siding on the small building at the back of the hotel is the only surviving usable part of the original Caribou Hotel

Stove unearthed from under the hotel in 2007 was probably from the original hotel and left buried in the sand after the fire in 1909

Firefighting technology had been improving but was still, for the most part, inadequate in the early years of the 20th century. Bucket lines, where residents lined up and passed buckets of water from hand to hand with the person at the front throwing it onto the flames, were still the main method of combatting fire in most small communities. Once a fire started it was almost impossible to extinguish and the most effective firefighting strategy was simply to try to contain it so it would destroy as small an area as possible.

Builders recognized the danger and started mitigating the risk by sheathing their structures in galvanized iron or tin, which would prevent sparks from a fire elsewhere from igniting the tinder dry wood underneath.

Colonel Conrad's house, still in use in 2019, was used as a temporary hotel after the fire and until the new hotel was built in 1910.

That may have been why the Yukon Hotel had been given galvanized iron siding when it was built in Bennett in 1899. The siding was still in place on the Caribou Hotel and on a small outbuilding, which was being used as the cookhouse for the restaurant.

December, 1909, was a mild month as far as northern winters are concerned. People were laying in small fires in their stoves just to keep the chill at bay.

Low-heat fires are in their own way just as dangerous as a roaring blaze. The chimney stays cooler and more creosote, one of the substances found in wood smoke, condenses on the inside of the metal as a sticky tar-like fuel and ignites into a chimney fire when a hotter blaze is built in the stove. Creosote also burns with a much more intense heat than wood, negating any protection the chimney may provide against the flames spreading.

It was just after 3 p.m. on Christmas Eve when someone noticed there was a fire in the attic of the Caribou. A group of men, including Alex Chisholm — who was probably a hotel guest since no one in Carcross seemed to know who he was — climbed to the roof of the hotel to see if they could tackle the flames from above. According to Chisholm, who was later interviewed by the Whitehorse Star, the men initially headed toward the chimney when the fire suddenly breached the roof several metres away from it. Realizing they were in danger of being trapped on the roof they retreated back down the stairs.

Down below, Edwin and Bessie Gideon had already recognized their hotel was going to burn and recruited anyone they could to help them salvage what they could and sent word to their neighbouring businesses.

Priorities might have been a little skewed by the fact that most of the recruits were guests or locals who had spent the early part of the afternoon in the bar.

The piano from the bar was rushed out the door. The pool tables followed behind. Then the woodstove. Some furniture from the kitchen and dining room and, finally, the entire inventory of the bar. Next door, George Fickhardt was able to save most of the stock from his grocery store.

Then all anyone could do was stand back and watch. It took one hour for the Caribou, the grocery store, the train depot, and Frank McPhee's general merchandise store to be, in Fickhardt's words, "wiped off the face of the earth." There were light winds that helped firefighters stop the spread of the flames and limit the damage to the four buildings.

Out on the street the Gideons were literally left only with the clothes on their backs. Their guests had lost all of their effects and the Japanese cook lost everything he owned including his life's savings, which had been hidden in his mattress. The only parts of the Caribou that hadn't burned were the galvanized steel cladding and the icebox from the kitchen. The cladding lay in heaps among the ashes.

Bessie and Edwin knew they couldn't waste time getting back into business. Part of Colonel Conrad's large house around the corner had originally been built as an office and bunkhouse in 1902 and by nightfall they had taken it over to give their paying guests shelter from the cold. Temperatures dropped to minus 40 degrees that night.

It took a little longer to get the bar reopened but they built a platform, put up a tent, and had the piano, pool tables, woodstove, and liquor sales back in operation in time to celebrate the New Year.

It was a good thing that Colonel Conrad wasn't around much over the next year. His Big Thing Mine was struggling and he was "outside" most of the time trying to find new financing to keep himself afloat. The Gideons operated the Caribou Hotel from his residence for the next 10 months.

McPhee and Fickhardt found temporary quarters from which to continue business and the WPYR converted an old unused section house into an interim depot and customs station.

Chapter 9

W. H. SIMPSON

When Jamie Toole and Anne Morgan purchased the Caribou Hotel in 2006, their plan was to restore it to the same condition as it was when re-opened by Bessie and Edwin Gideon in October, 1910.

In 1910, Bessie and Edwin had no intention of letting their new business disappear because of the inconvenience of a fire. Living in Colonel Conrad's house brought them in contact with Jack Stewart – a former sparring partner for world heavyweight boxing champion "Gentleman Jim" Corbett and the owner of a freight-hauling business that had most of its business with Conrad's mines on Montana Mountain. He agreed to bankroll the rebuilding of the hotel which, when completed, cost approximately $14,000.

They negotiated a new lease with Annie Auston. The Gideons would own the hotel structure but Annie would retain ownership of the land.

Architect J.J. Killam was contracted to provide them with the blueprints for a lodging that would be a modern day marvel for hotels – encompassing the latest in building techniques, technology, and design.

The potbelly woodstove in the bar, previously the main source of warmth for the entire building, would now only be for show. The new main source of heat was a large wood-burning furnace in the crawl space beneath the foundation. Lights were both brilliant and economic, replacing kerosene lamps and candles with gasoline burners. It claimed to have hot bathes and running water – although where the running water came from is anyone's guess since plumbing wasn't installed in the hotel until 1942. On the hotel's exterior the windows had elegant canopies over each one to shade patrons from the direct sunlight.

There were 20 rooms on the top two floors and they shared a common washroom and toilet on each floor. An owner's suite on the second floor, where the Gideons lived, had its own bathroom.

When completed the Caribou was the kind of first-class accommodation, restaurant, and bar that one could expect to find in any major metropolis in the world in the early 1900s.

In 2006, Jamie Toole and Anne Morgan decided that hotel was the one they wanted to recreate. "We want this building to be finished off beautifully," said Jamie. "When people and customers walk in here, (they'll) be stepping back 100 years in time."

And it was about then William H. Simpson came back.

William was the Whitehorse-based carpentry contractor the Gideons hired to build the new Caribou in 1910. When the job was completed he returned to Whitehorse and although he may have visited from time to time while still alive there is no record he ever worked again in Carcross nor is there a record of when he passed away.

Rather than cutting new lumber for the hotel William went to Conrad City and searched for salvageable material from abandoned buildings. While most gold rush towns turn into debris Carcross seemed to thrive on collecting the remains from other failed communities to ensure it kept on growing.

Many of the existing buildings in Carcross were pulled or floated across the lakes from Bennett and Conrad City. Frank McPhee's general merchandise store next door to the Caribou included the Vendome Hotel – dragged over the ice from Bennett in the spring of 1911 by Jack Stewart – in its reconstruction. Those that were completely rebuilt without adding existing structures, like the Caribou, were mostly constructed using recycled lumber.

Patsy Henderson (L) and Jack Stewart c1948. Jack financed the rebuilding of the Caribou Hotel in 1910

There wasn't much useful material he could salvage from Conrad so most of the hotel was built with Pine and Spruce lumber from King's Sawmill and massive Fir studs and joists purchased in southern BC and hauled in on the railroad. The chimney bricks were made by craftsmen in Carcross. The icebox and metal cladding that survived the fire were put back in the kitchen and hung on the walls and roof of the cookhouse respectively.

Under the corners of the new structure he placed four massive granite stones to act as a foundation to provide some stability to the structure because the ground under it was made of sand as far as anyone could dig.

In 2006, Jamie decided he wanted to reuse as much of the old material as he could, especially the Fir. It doesn't deteriorate because most of the insects and weather conditions that affect it elsewhere aren't present in the north. In fact, it seems to get more dense and stronger with age.

Board from window frame in hotel with Mrs. Gideon's name written on it

He and Anne picked through the hotel and discovered William H. Simpson's name scrawled everywhere on the backs of boards. "WHS Carcross" and "Simpson" were the two most common they came across. Some they left in place because they could be recycled. Those they couldn't use were put into storage. Other boards had Bessie and Edwin's names written on them.

Restoration is as much about forensic carpentry as it is about building something. Everything tells a story.

Jamie noticed there were nails in a piece of wood that theoretically shouldn't have nails in it because it was covered by a supporting beam. The only explanation was that the beam had been added at a later date to prevent the hotel from collapsing in on itself.

They determined the kitchen, which many old-timers claimed to have been added at a later date, did in fact date from 1910. It still had both the original galvanized cladding on it, although it was a lot rustier now, and the icebox from the first Caribou Hotel.

An area they opened up in the front entryway revealed that the original interior colors of the hotel walls were pink, yellow, and white.

As they removed old lathe from the walls inside the hotel they found that Smith and his workers apparently had a habit of occasionally stapling the dates on the backs of material when they constructed certain areas.

Jamie found the date "Monday, Dec. 26" stapled on the mortar under the lathe siding on one wall. Using a calendar he figured out that Dec. 26 was a Monday in 1910.

Which suggests, while the hotel opened for business in October 1910 of that year, final construction probably wasn't complete until at least early 1911.

However, it appears that when you recreate the past you sometimes stir it up as well.

It was during a quiet afternoon while working in the Caribou that Jamie and Anne first heard the hammering coming from a floor above them.

They looked at each other in confusion. There was, as far as they knew, nobody else in the building.

Caribou Hotel reconstruction began in 2006

"Did you lock the door?" asked Anne. Jamie nodded.

"Then who is that?"

The two of them crept out of the restaurant and slowly went up the stairs. Before they reached the top, the banging stopped. They waited, but there was only silence.

It happened again and again until it became a regular feature of their work in the Caribou. When they were by themselves the hammering would start, then quit when they went looking for its source. No matter how stealthy and quiet they tried to be it never failed to cease before they got to it. They told their workers about it so they wouldn't be spooked if it happened while they were working there.

One afternoon Jamie had his crew working in the bar area. The flooring in front of the bar was mostly worn down by 100 years of patrons' boots and spilled booze. Holes eventually opened up in the flooring but rather than replacing the wood, previous owners simply nailed tin can lids over the gaps. The workers removed most of the lids in preparation for working on the floor.

One of the carpenters glanced down through one of the openings and there was a man in the basement looking up at him, who then turned and walked away into the darkness. He had just been down in the basement, knew there was nobody there, and the man was definitely not someone he recognized.

"That's too much. I'm outa here," he announced to Jamie and their co-workers. He didn't even bother picking up his tool belt which was sitting on the bar beside him – just charged for the door.

"It was a man he saw, not a woman, so it wasn't Mrs. Gideon. We're pretty sure it was W.H.," said Anne in 2017. "We hear the hammering all the time and we think it's him doing the work. But when you're the only ones in the building it does get your pulse racing and your curiosity going.

"'When he appeared in the basement...we think he was checking up on the new foundation under the hotel to make sure it's up to his standards."

Chapter 10

BESSIE
DEAD
AND
ALIVE

It's odd that there is more information about what Bessie Gideon did (and apparently still does) after her death on Oct. 27, 1933, than there is for when she was alive.

Edwin died on Oct. 27, 1925, but never came back. He was buried in the pioneer cemetery on the south side of the narrows.

Bessie's funeral was held in Carcross and she was definitely buried there – but where? There is no known gravesite for her and a search in 1995 failed to uncover any evidence of where one might be. Possibly that is why her ethereal presence still hangs around the Caribou. A plaque was placed beside Edwin's headstone in 2010 but it doesn't appear to have settled her spirit.

Since passing away she has been described in local, national, and international media as being a kind-hearted but shy or timid spirit who knocks on doors, puts bubbles in people's bathtubs or simply watches people from a third-storey window of the hotel. One guest helped a little old lady down the stairs and out the front door because he thought she had accidently been locked in the building and couldn't get out – except that it turned out there was no little old lady, just Bessie.

Bessie, Edwin and Louise Dawson

Occasionally, she even helped with the housekeeping and knew how to operate an electric vacuum cleaner.

Other experiences were more personal but equally benign.

In the 1990s a cook, Kathy Haydon, frequently heard her name being called from other areas of the hotel. When she went to find out what was wanted, she found only an empty room or that no one in the place had called for her. It became a source of amusement for her co-workers.

Bartender Janet Thompson occasionally slept at the hotel after her late-night shift ended and was sometimes awakened in the middle of the night. She had long brown hair and would open her eyes to find it standing straight up above her head. Then, after a moment, the hair was dropped back onto her face.

Kind-hearted, harmless, and shy or not, it's still a chilling and terrifying experience to encounter a ghost for the first time but neither woman quit their job. After awhile they figured that Bessie and her antics were just part of working at the Caribou.

After 80 years of prowling the halls and rooms of the Caribou the post-life Bessie became so famous that, in 2015, Canada Post issued a ghoulish stamp with what they envisioned was her skeletal likeness hovering ominously over the hotel. The Caribou itself is constantly listed in travel guides and on social media as one of the more fascinating haunted hotels in North America and Bessie, cited as its preeminent soul.

Details about the Gideons before the Caribou are sparse. They were from Illinois. Her name before getting married was Bessie Geraldine Trusty and she has been described as a "little bit of a thing." Edwin was born in 1862, the youngest of six brothers. They were married before they tackled the Chilkoot Trail as part of the Gold Rush stampede in 1898 — which made her one of the few women to come into Canada's north by that route at that time (of the approximately 40,000 souls who tackled the Chilkoot Trail in 1897-98, just over 1,000 were female).

They either liked what they found in the Yukon or didn't find enough and couldn't afford to leave since the next reference to them is seven years later when they were operating the Canyon Roadhouse near Kluane Lake.

It is possible Dawson Charlie stayed at their roadhouse since he and Skookum Jim were prospecting in the area that year. If the Gideons met the two men in 1905 then that may have been when they heard about Carcross and the Caribou Hotel. The Gideons also operated the Braeburn Roadhouse, a stop on the stage road between Whitehorse and Dawson City, over the winter of 1906-07.

When they leased the Caribou from Annie Auston in 1908 they brought with them their experience from the Canyon Roadhouse and Braeburn. The fire on Christmas Eve a year into their lease provided them with an opportunity and a fresh start to put those skills to their best use.

What became quickly apparent after the fire was that Edwin and Bessie understood the value of being good hosts, were charming, made friends easily, were community oriented and shrewd businesspeople.

The hotel they were building was, as the Whitehorse Star phrased it, "in advance of the town at the present time" and they were already looking past the southern lakes' mining communities to find new bodies to fill their beds.

For the grand re-opening on October 21, 1910, they arranged for a special train – the first ever chartered railroad excursion on the WPYR – to bring selected guests from Whitehorse for the party.

The train arrived in Carcross at 9:15 that night and was greeted at the station by almost the entire population of both Carcross and Conrad City who escorted them to the hotel. A veteran terpsichorean, H.W. Vance, called the steps as the revellers danced the night away.

Dinner was served just after midnight and the partying went on until the early hours of the morning, finally concluding with a rousing rendition of "Jolly Good Fellows" paying tribute to the Gideons and their top-shelf hospitality.

They followed up the grand opening with a Christmas Eve dinner and dance for the ore haulers and miners who were frequent customers.

The hotel, the replacement train station across the railroad tracks, and Frank McPhee's reconstructed store next door weren't the only changes in Carcross and the southern lakes in those years.

The mining industry in the southern lakes region was struggling for survival and that didn't bode well for businesses like the Caribou – but

S.S. Tutshi docked at Carcross. Caribou Hotel can be seen with the Scott Hotel just behind it

new business opportunities were starting to appear so the Gideon's vision of looking further abroad for customers was well suited to the times.

The Conrad mines on Montana Mountain had been promoted as a sure thing for investors and, in 1906, it looked like it would live up to its promise. However, a report by geologist Joseph Tyrrell, who understood that mining was as much about promotion and speculation as it was about results, declared the claims to be essentially worthless. He suggested that Colonel Conrad himself was an incompetent manager.

The Colonel's financing disappeared almost overnight, production at the mine slowed to a trickle, and people started to leave Conrad City.

Conrad managed to persuade other investors to get involved in 1908 and the mine ramped up its activity again, but it was always tenuous because of the low-grade ore and the Colonel spent most of his time "outside" looking for more financing. Miners continued to move away in search of job security elsewhere. When the postmaster in Conrad City died in 1909 the post office didn't bother to replace him and closed its building there permanently in 1910.

Caribou Hotel with Bessie standing on the balcony with Polly on her shoulder

In 1912, the Colonel declared bankruptcy and two years later there was only one resident, an elderly woman, left in Conrad City.

When a mountainside collapsed at Ben-My-Chree in 1911 burying the mine under a ton of rubble and killing Stanley McLellan – one of the partners in the gold claims – along with his wife Anne, Otto and Kate Partridge decided they had had enough.

The demise of the mines at Ben-My-Chree and Conrad City left only one operating mine, the Engineer Mine on Taku Arm, in a district that once had been touted as the future centre of mining and development in the north.

However, a new industry was just starting to grow. Even though they were finished with mining Kate and Otto were reluctant to leave their paradise at the south end of Taku Arm.

Along with a friend of Kate's, Emily Dalton, and another of Otto's partners in the mine, Ludwig Swanson, they decided to turn their homestead into a luxury resort and market it to their well-heeled acquaintances and socially elite friends and family in Britain and the United States.

What they sold to potential visitors was the mystique of the "Northern Alps" – a deep blue glacier serving as a backdrop to fields of gardens and flowers surrounded by towering snow-capped peaks and a turquoise-coloured lake, frequented by moose, bears, wolves, and mountain goats.

Kate played a portable organ, which she claimed to have carried on her back over the Chilkoot Trail in 1898, for sing-alongs and dances. Otto, a captivating storyteller, spun tales of the gold rush while visitors dined on gourmet meals and sipped their famous home-made rhubarb wine. Despite the arduous journey to get there, at its peak Ben-My-Chree hosted up to 9,000 of the rich and famous every summer.

It wasn't an easy trip nor a fast one. One had to travel by boat up the coast from Vancouver or Seattle, take the train from Skagway to Carcross, then board the Gleaner churning its way down the lake. The Gleaner was dry-docked for repairs in 1918 and never refloated. It was replaced by the Tutshi (Tlingit name meaning Black Lake), which ferried people to Ben-My-Chree until 1955. It could take nearly a month for a visitor from Europe to reach their destination.

Among their guests were the former President of the United States, Teddy Roosevelt, international opera star soprano Alma Gluck, many members of the British House of Lords, various Governor Generals of Canada, a multitude of movie stars (including, in the 1930s, Clark Gable and Robert Taylor) and Edward, Prince of Wales – the future King of England who abdicated from the British throne in 1937 to be with the woman he loved. There is no record that Bessie Warfield (later better known as Wallis-Simpson, the woman he loved) was ever at Ben-My-Chree.

Almost all of them overnighted at Carcross. The Caribou became part of their experience, either because they spent the night there or simply swilled beer in the bar.

Tourism was already starting to make its mark before Ben-My-Chree became a major destination.

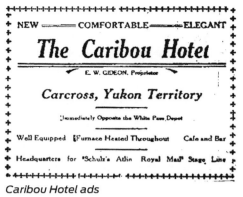

Rather than fading from public memory the Klondike Gold Rush was actually growing in popularity, helped no doubt by the writings of poet Robert Service, novelist Rex Beach, journalist Tappan Adney, the "Poet of the Sierras" Joaquin Miller, and short-story writer Jack London among numerous others. People always long for an untamed frontier and the Yukon and Alaska fit the bill. They had heard about the Klondike Gold Rush, now they wanted to come and see what it was all about.

Every tourist who came to the Yukon had to spend time in Carcross because the WPYR was still the only way to get into the north.

The fledgling Alaska cruise ship industry was persuaded to stop in Skagway for two days to enable passengers to ride the railroad to Carcross one day, stay overnight, and return the next. By 1926, the summertime tourism industry was booming enough that the waiting room in the WPYR station was enlarged and the lake steamer Tutshi retrofitted to increase the number of passengers it could carry.

The Tutshi had a sailing schedule it was supposed to adhere to but it wasn't unusual for sailings to be delayed for a day or two due to weather or repairs. All the passengers could do was take a room in the Caribou and sit in the bar waiting to be summoned by the steamship crew.

In the early 1930s, the last surviving person who had been in the Klondike when gold was discovered in 1896, Patsy Henderson, started entertaining tourists at the train station with stories, displays, and dance – telling of the traditional lifestyle of the Tagish, the discovery of gold, and the change that followed. He would continue to educate and entertain visitors for four decades.

It was one of Otto Partridge's partners in the Ben-My-Chree mining venture, Lord Maurice Egerton, who helped kick off another industry. The British aristocrat was an avid big game hunter and preferred hunting in the north to safaris in Africa. Big game hunting was pretty much the private sanctum of the wealthy and there were affluent Britons and Americans who were willing and able to spend whatever it cost to bag themselves a trophy.

Big game hunters comprised a relatively small but international community. They liked to write about their hunts in books and magazines, in particular, Charles Sheldon, the "Father of Denali National Park", who wrote a number of books about hunting in the Yukon and Alaska. Between Sheldon and Egerton it didn't take long for the word to get out – the Yukon had big game and plenty of it.

Because they knew the land and understood the animals, Indigenous people were hired to guide the hunters. They thought it was a little strange that people would pay so much to hunt an animal that they went out to harvest every year for subsistence. However, weird work was better than no work they reasoned. They were getting paid to let someone else do the hunting for them – the hunter took his trophy and the guide got the meat. As long as they didn't laugh at the hunter, they were told, it was easy work for them.

By 1907 there were three established outfitters in the Carcross area. In 1917, an 18-year old Indigenous man named Johnnie Johns decided to open his own hunting business. To do it he had also to relinquish his "Indian" status because Indians weren't allowed to own an outfitting business.

Over the next five decades it was he who put Carcross on the world map as a sportsman's destination and established the Caribou as the place to stay when in town.

Millie Jones (McMurphy) and Jamie Toole placing Bessie's marker at Edwin's gravesite in the Carcross cemetery

While tourism and hunters filled the hotel for six months of the year there were still six months of winter when the only bed business was train crews being put up overnight by the WPYR and a dwindling number of freighters who carried ore from the mines. Train passengers spent their time huddled in the hotel café trying to stay warm and waiting for the locomotive's whistle to call them to re-board. They had a snack, drank coffee, some spent time in the bar but few rented rooms.

One had to be creative to generate revenue during the lean winter months.

The Gideons served as agents for local outfitters and trappers. The hide of a silver tipped grizzly bear covered one wall of the hotel lounge and another room hung with wolf pelts ready for sale. The headquarters for the Royal Mail Stage to Atlin was the hotel's reception desk. They held bingos once a week and dances as often as they could. At Christmas, they and the Scott Hotel hosted a turkey shoot followed by dinner and a dance. They hosted weddings, anniversaries, birthday parties, whist and crib tournaments – anything to get people out of their cabins and have them walk through blowing snow, ice fog, and bone-chilling cold to take part in the festivities.

And the locals came because, other than northern lights, dog mushing, snowshoeing, and skiing, it was the only show in town.

Bessie and Edwin also realized that aviation, although no planes had yet flown into the Yukon, was something that had the potential to change the north and provide them with the type of business opportunity they enjoyed. They hosted a party on the roof of the Caribou so people could watch the De Havilland DH-4s of the US Army's Black Wolf Squadron fly over on their landmark New York to Nome journey in August, 1920 – a journey to demonstrate to the world aviation community the practicality of long-distance travel. Not until 1928 when the Queen of the Yukon, sister ship to Charles Lindberg's Spirit of St. Louis, landed on the airstrip did that vision come true for Carcross.

A canoe downstream of the railway bridge across the narrows

Chapter 11

WATER UNDER THE BRIDGE

Prohibition is never a hotel's best friend — especially in the north where fiscal survival often relies on booze sales during the long northern winter.

When Prohibition was declared in the Yukon the Northwest Mounted Police apparently marched into the Caribou Hotel and seized its liquor stock. Their orders were to destroy it so they carried cases of beer, wine, and hard liquor onto the WPYR bridge and used the iron rails to break the neck off each bottle so they could pour its contents into the narrows below.

Local lore has Skookum Jim paddling a canoe out into the narrows downstream of the bridge and dropping anchor. He held a cup in his hand, which he used to dip into the water to capture the alcohol before it got too diluted.

According to the story, he didn't really want or need the alcohol; he just wanted to have some fun with the constabulary. Prohibition prohibited the drinking of alcohol and, for Skookum Jim, so did the Indian Act. But they couldn't put him in jail for drinking water out of the river.

This photo of the Northwest Mounted Police may have led to the myth of Skookum Jim and the breaking of bottles on the railway bridge during prohibition. The police are destroying alcohol for some unknown reason and pouring it into the river from the bridge, but this occurred in 1909 – prohibition was declared in 1918

So he sat in the canoe, dipping his cup, and taking one drink after another. It was fun, he allegedly conceded, but in truth it was mostly pure water with very little flavour.

It is probably a rural myth.

Someone may indeed have anchored themselves downstream from the bridge and drank copious amounts of river water mixed with alcohol, but it wasn't Skookum Jim.

He died in 1916. Prohibition didn't come to the Yukon until 1918.

Bessie and Louise stand under the Caribou's beer sign in the early 1930s

But it makes an amusing tale with a recognizable name – the storytellers reason – so why let facts ruin a good yarn.

There was a plebiscite held in 1916, which was narrowly won by "the Drys" (those who favoured a sober, morally pure society) but the territorial government decided not to declare Prohibition. Not until the federal government instituted a short-lived ban on alcohol in 1918 did Temperance become the law of the land. Prohibition in the Yukon lasted only as long as it took for the territorial government, handcuffed by cutbacks to funding from the federal government in Ottawa, to realize that without the revenue generated by alcohol sales they would soon be broke.

In 1921, another plebiscite was won by "the Wets" (those who favoured a debauched society soaked with demon drink) and Prohibition in the Yukon was repealed.

It was the shortest period of prohibition for any jurisdiction in the world but it didn't solve the alcohol shortage in the Yukon. For booze to reach the Yukon it had to go through Alaska via the WPYR. There was no ground link directly south to Canada. The United States had adopted Prohibition in January, 1920, and wouldn't allow alcohol to be shipped through American territory to the Yukon.

Yukoners came up with all sorts of ideas to get around the Americans including flying beer up in an aircraft – a radical plan that prompted the US Congress to invent and pass into law for the first time the concept of "air sovereignty" – where the US could extend their jurisdiction for enforcing laws "upward in the air indefinitely over American territory" to prevent such flights passing over their land.

Not until 1924 was an agreement reached between the American and Canadian governments to lift the blockade on alcohol shipments through Alaska to the Yukon.

There is also evidence to suggest the breaking of the bottles on the bridge never actually took place. Apparently, when Prohibition arrived Yukon bars were allowed to continue selling alcohol until their inventory ran out. They just couldn't buy any more to replenish their stock.

Reginald Brooks recalled meeting three mining engineers at the train depot in Carcross in early October, 1918 – six months after the national declaration of Prohibition.

"Is there a bar here?" was the first question asked by Clarence Wilson. He was one of the three sent to inspect Engineer Mine by the Mining Corporation of Canada, which was negotiating to purchase the claims from Captain James Alexander.

They went across to the Caribou Hotel and settled down in the bar for a few drinks.

"I'm from Ontario," explained Clarence, "and to take a drink there...one has to act like a criminal. To take a drink here is like being in a free country for a while."

Reginald had a good reason to remember the dates and details when writing his personal history of the Engineer Mine many years later. It was one of the last times he saw those three men alive. Their fate, and Captain Alexander's linked together for eternity.

Chapter 12

REQUIEM

The Yukon government granted special dispensation for him to be buried in the Carcross Pioneer Cemetery when he died in 1972 at the estimated age of 125. What else could they do for one who had cheated death and gone on to achieve international infamy?

Dignitaries filled a special train from Whitehorse and, after arriving in Carcross, spent a number of hours sitting in the Caribou waiting for the funeral to begin. The hotel put on a buffet lunch and visitors mingled with locals eating, drinking, and reminiscing.

They proudly displayed the scars that he had given them. Others talked of how different operatic arias sounded when he gave voice to them with his unique vocal chords – a music that stopped all conversation in the room as people shut up to listen. A few recalled his hymn singing.

Most spoke about his offensive language, saying he couldn't have learned his vocabulary from miners or sailors since he was so much more foulmouthed than they. Of his drinking, they said, there was nothing worse than a reformed drunk.

When the time came a funeral procession of cars and pickup trucks assembled on the street in front of the hotel. He was retrieved from

Polly's Funeral. Johnnie Johns can be seen in the center of the photo wearing his treasured hat with his drum on the ground beside him

the hotel freezer where he had spent the last two months since dying, placed in the red velvet-lined coffin built just for him, and carefully set in the back of one of the trucks with all the ceremony accorded a royal dignitary.

The procession slowly weaved its way through Carcross's few streets then crossed over to the south side where it was diverted through the residences there and finally down the dirt road to the cemetery. Those who weren't in the procession came out of their homes, lining the side of the road to pay homage as he was driven past. Some then followed it on foot.

The coffin was placed above the grave and mourners huddled together for warmth in the cold evening air and snow. Retired hunting guide Johnnie Johns gave the eulogy during the graveside ceremony. He wore a 300-year old swansdown hat on a leather backing – an heirloom he had never previously displayed in public – in honour of his old friend with whom he had shared so many hours of spinning tales and entertaining in the Caribou café over the past five decades.

"Dog is known as man's best friend," he said, "But Polly was the best friend of many people in Carcross, especially the children. There is probably a dog world for dogs that died and also a Polly world for parrots who died."

Then he sang "I Love You Truly" – a 1901 parlour song for weddings, not apt for a funeral but it had been Polly's favorite.

"Life with its sorrow, life with its tear," he crooned with tears running down his aged face and the mourners wept with him. "Fades into dreams when I feel you are near...."

Then, as the coffin was slowly lowered into the grave, Johnnie bade him farewell with a traditional Tagish song accompanied by a skin drum.

When the service was over everyone filed back to the Caribou and the drinking began. Hotel owner Dorothy Hopcott spent hours reading the hundreds of telegrams and letters from hunters, celebrities, tourists, miners, and journalists from around the world who wanted to share tales of their experiences with him and their sorrow at his loss.

She spoke of the morning she found him on the bottom of the cage, mimicking with her facial expression and arms what a parrot looks like when lying on its back with its legs sticking straight up.

She had often found him lying on his back like that, she said, but he could usually be roused with a gentle finger poke. That morning he hadn't responded when poked.

"We decided we were going to have a great wake in his honour," she explained to the crowd, "So we put him in the freezer and organized this celebration."

Polly's headstone in the Carcross cemetery

The day he died CBC Radio was notified and was preparing a short broadcast to the nation when they discovered an aspiring Carcross artist was having an art show in Vancouver. CBC contacted Ted Harrison, spoke with him about Polly, and produced a longer piece for their public affairs radio.

Ted had been unaware of Polly's death until contacted by the CBC. When the interview was over he set up his easel in the Vancouver hotel room and whipped up a painting of Polly, which he added to the show. The painting sold along with all the others and is in a private collection somewhere.

The mourners listened, reminisced, ate from a buffet, and drank a lot.

Polly's replacement – a chatty Mexican parrot named Hombre, donated by CFCF Radio from Montreal, Quebec, and flown across Canada by CP Air – was introduced and promptly renamed Polly ll. Another replacement, a massive Macaw named Scarlet O'Hara, turned up a day or so later sent by a woman from Victoria, BC.

Scarlet, the woman told Dorothy, had been on the British Battle cruiser H.M.S. Hood when it docked in Victoria, BC, during its 1923-24 global circumnavigation but the ship's captain didn't particularly like the foulmouthed bird. He unloaded Scarlet onto the donor who tolerated her for almost 50 years before deciding she would be a fitting successor for Polly. The "Mighty Hood" was sunk during a shoot-out with the German Battleship Bismark in 1941.

A spruce replica of Polly was also given to the hotel by carver Gary Sam. A third parrot arrived a couple of years later and was named Ombre.

The wake went on until the early hours of the morning and the hangovers lasted well into the next day.

A brass plaque was later placed over his resting place.

"Underneath this sod lies a sourdough parrot
Its heart was gold, pure fourteen carat
Polly now can spread her wings
Leaving behind all earthly things

Chapter 13

POLLY

Nobody knows why the male Yellow-naped Amazon parrot was called Polly. Possibly because it's claimed to be impossible to know what sex a parrot is until it comes time to lay an egg...or not...by which time he had already been named and his owner wasn't about to change his or her mind.

Speculation abounds about how Polly got into the Yukon, where he was before coming north, and how old he was when he arrived but that's all it is – speculation. His headstone bears a birthdate of 1850, but there are no records to support it.

What is known is that he lived at Engineer Mine with Captain James and Louise Alexander prior to 1913. Starting that year James and Louise decided to spend their winters out of the Yukon, usually in Vancouver, BC, where the climate was a little milder and snow less common. At the end of October each year they traveled to Carcross with Polly and their dog – an English Setter who apparently didn't have a name.

They dropped Polly off with Bessie and Edwin Gideon and continued, with the dog, on their journey south. He spent the winter in the Caribou and

Polly being held by Louise Alexander at Engineer Mine. Reginald Brooks is far left. Captain Alexander is seated on the stool. This is the only known photograph of the dog that survived the sinking of the S.S. Sophia in October, 1918. It can be seen beside the man sitting on the deck behind Captain Alexander

when the Alexanders returned in the spring went with them to Engineer Mine for the summer.

That pattern was already going to change even before the events of Oct. 23-25, 1918, determined the fates of Polly and everyone involved with him.

James decided to sell Engineer Mine at the end of the 1917 mining season – he was getting older and the demands of the war in Europe had drained the available work force. Each year it got harder and harder to find miners to work in the north and his heart just wasn't in it any more.

While in Vancouver the winter of 1917-18 he entered into negotiations with the Mining Corporation of Canada and the following spring there was a million dollar deal on the table. The only thing left to finalize the sale was for the purchaser to inspect the property – which is why Reginald Brooks picked up those three mining engineers in Carcross in early October, 1918.

The three inspectors sent a positive report to their employer and the Alexanders decided to return with them to Vancouver a week or so earlier than they normally did to expedite the final paperwork.

While sitting in the Caribou visiting with the Gideons they talked of the future. There was a large home they were planning to build in Vancouver,

Polly

an island they wanted to purchase in the Strait of Georgia, and a yacht to ferry them between the two and probably further abroad on the Pacific Ocean.

When they and the three engineers boarded the train for Skagway the Alexanders left Polly behind as they usually did. From Skagway they sailed for Vancouver on the Canadian Pacific luxury liner Princess Sophia on Oct. 23. Whether or not they were intending to make one final trip back to Engineer Mine and to retrieve their beloved bird in the spring of 1919 is unknown.

That night, in high seas and a blinding snowstorm, the ship struck Vanderbilt Reef close to its first port of call in Juneau, Alaska. For 40 hours she sat on top of the rock surrounded by rescue vessels unable to reach her. In the late afternoon of Oct. 25, 1918, the Princess Sophia slid off the reef and sank to the bottom of the Lynn Canal in history's worst marine disaster on North America's West coast. By daylight of October 26, only her foremast remained when the storm abated and the USS Cedar who had stood vigil all night drew near to find all souls had been lost. Of the 298 passengers, 65 crew, an unknown number of Chinese workers who allegedly were below deck but not listed on the manifest, 25 horses and five dogs, there was only one survivor – the Alexander's English Setter. The dog never returned to the Yukon.

Louise Dawson, Bessie Gideon and Polly

Polly, denied a life of luxury in the big house in Vancouver, was destined to end his days in a small hotel in northern Canada. He was a curiosity at first – the bird who cheated death because he had been left behind, but it didn't take long to show there was more to this bird than dumb luck.

Bessie placed his cage in the café, on a table close to the door leading into the bar and he quickly developed a taste for scotch. Bar patrons, mostly miners, sneaked over from the bar and poured drinks into the water bowl in the bottom of the cage. He drank until he fell off his perch and passed out lying on his back with his legs sticking into the air, snoring softly.

Drunks staggered up to his cage and shoved soggy crackers through the bars. Contrary to popular belief, parrots don't really like crackers – especially ones that have been soaked in beer or whiskey. Their preferred diet is fruit, nuts, and vegetables. Polly didn't appreciate the food being offered by the miners.

In the future, whenever people approached his cage and asked, "Polly want a cracker?" he mostly responded, "Go to hell!" When one was offered to him he would grab it, break it up with his beak, and spit it out.

At some point in his pre-hotel life someone played a lot of opera music and he memorized arias from various pieces. Occasionally, he burst into song, his distinctive voice bringing a unique dimension to the works of the operatic masters. Conversation in the café and bar stopped when he performed as the customers listened in amazement.

Opera wasn't the only musical genre in his repertoire. He also sang family-oriented parlour songs, especially "I Love You Truly", and ribald bar ditties that would make a sailor blush.

He had a vocabulary that Canadian Press journalist Dennis Bell, in 1972, wrote helped make "The world famous Carcross parrot...the oldest, meanest, ugliest bird north of the 60th parallel" and resulted in Whitehorse riverboat captain Henry Breaden calling Polly "the dirty devil with the bad mouth."

When people poked their finger through the bars trying to touch him he didn't hesitate to try to take the end of the digit off with a single snap of his beak. Even if he didn't succeed in completely severing the fingertip, just drawing blood from his tormenters gave him immense pleasure. He strutted, chattered, and preened while people scurried around trying to find a bandage to patch the wound. The unique triangular shape of the scar became a badge of honour for those privileged enough to be bitten.

He didn't like dogs, cats or other birds either.

About the only things Polly seemed to tolerate were children and the mirror in his cage, although he regurgitated onto it every day.

Johnnie Johns's outfitting business was starting to thrive in the 1920s and he made sure his highbrow, wealthy clientele from around the world not only stayed in a Caribou Hotel room but ate at least one meal in the café during their stopover in Carcross. Breaking bread with Polly, he believed, was an experience without any pretense of social graces that no one should be denied.

While dining on simple café fare they listened to Polly imitate the meows of a cat, rip off a string of profanity, belt out an aria, rattle off a colourful ditty, and croon "I Love You Truly" or "Springtime in the Rockies." For the Gideons and Johnnie Johns it was better than serving a gourmet meal with all the fancy trappings and hiring a professional piano player.

Johnnie's clients seemed to agree. Polly's reputation spread beyond the Yukon through word of mouth and the international media touting him, and the Caribou, as a destination for tourists. When the train rolled into

Carcross each day passengers scrambled to get out of their railcars and into the hotel to spend time with the parrot. Newspapers and magazines sent their travel writers into the north with instructions to stop in Carcross and send a story back on their time with a bird that most southern journalists believed was nothing more than a myth to be debunked.

Being a somewhat religious woman Bessie decided Polly needed to be converted. As much as she liked having the parrot as the main attraction in town and knew the colourful vocabulary was part of his charm, she felt his language wasn't appropriate for a family-oriented establishment.

She started by cutting off his liquor supply. Anyone caught pouring alcohol into the cage was banished from the hotel. It worked. Polly stopped drinking and proved there is truth in the old adage that, where booze is concerned, there's nothing like a rehabilitated alcoholic. Not only did he turn his beak up at the hint of a drink but he developed an intense dislike of anyone who smelled of sweat and spirits – whether the person was inebriated or not. Just the smell was enough to set him off.

With less time spent drinking he started singing more so Bessie started adding hymns into his repertoire. After a while the profanity, arias, and ditties were interspersed with verses from the "Battle Hymn of the Republic" and "Amazing Grace".

When the blasphemy got too much for her she covered the cage with a black blanket. For most parrots, darkness is enough to stop their chatter. For Polly covering the cage was like pushing a play button and cranking up the volume – but only for the first few minutes before he finally clammed up.

It wasn't all music and vulgarity. When Polly didn't feel like talking, he wouldn't say nor sing a word. Occasionally, he simply repeated snippets of conversations, sounds, and words he heard frequently. He could meow like a cat. During bingo games, the caller would call out the number, then Polly echoed the call, "Under the oh, sixty-six – oh, clickety click."

If parrots can be said to have a sense of humour, Polly displayed his on occasion.

Whitehorse resident Donna Clayson spent many summer afternoons in the hotel café feasting on ice cream when she was a teenager.

"One hot July day, four of us were at the restaurant and "ignoring" the four boys at another table. Every so often we would hear a whistle and "Look at those legs!" We all had shorts on and felt pretty good that the boys were noticing. When the boys got up and left and we still heard the soft whistle and "Look at those legs!" we were all embarrassed when we realized we were actually flirting with a parrot."

His rancour seemed to be aimed at adults. Where children were involved, he stopped swearing and singing and his entire demeanour changed. As a child growing up in Carcross, Hollie Smith had a long-term relationship with Polly and recalled his "mumbling love chatter" in her unpublished memoir, Evolution of a Scallywag.

"He'd latch onto the bars using his beak and feet to deftly slide down to the bottom of his cage," she wrote, "Incoherently muttering as he waddled over to me. I thought he was saying the equivalent of, 'Psst...kid, come over here. I got something secret I wanna tell ya'.... Occasionally he'd stop to fix me with one of his wee beady eyes, before striking the bars of his cage with his beak to make some important point.... Sometimes, if I listened real hard, it felt like I could understand his odd mutterings."

Hollie was one of the few people who could touch Polly without him trying to turn her fingers into a meal. Bessie Gideon was another. There are several photographs of Bessie standing outside the hotel with Polly perched on her shoulder.

Polly became part of the curriculum for students at the Chout'la Indian Residential School. This school was established by Anglican Bishop Bompas in 1901 on the south side of the narrows then a new school was built on the north side in 1911 by the Canadian Government. It was operated by the Anglican Church until 1969.

In the 1960s the teachers at the school told the story of how Polly came to live at the Caribou. On Saturdays they took groups of the children to the hotel to meet Polly and talk with him.

During those visits they likely also encountered Polly's friend – the great "Indian Scout" himself – Johnnie Johns, who was a café and bar regular and as author and sportsman John Batten wrote in his book The Forest and The Plain, "perhaps the world's...most famous hunter."

Johnnie Johns (R) and local children on the White Pass and Yukon Route Royal Mail stagecoach

Chapter 14

JOHNNIE JOHNS

Johnnie was used to being underestimated.

He was an "Indian" in a time when Indigenous people were considered wards of the government rather than citizens – governed by an Act of Parliament, the 1876 Indian Act and its various amendments, which spelled out their rights and restrictions. The aim of the legislation was, according to Canada's first Prime Minister, John A. Macdonald in 1887, "to do away with the tribal system and assimilate the Indian people in all respects with the other inhabitants of the Dominion."

People of European origin (Europeans, Canadians, Americans) tended to view Indigenous people as inferior, poor, uneducated, and unsuccessful with no motivation to change that fate simply because they weren't white.

Johnnie didn't see his race as an obstacle.

"I'm an Indian and you're not," he said in a 1980s conversation with Yukon journalist Don Sawatsky, "but that is an accident of birth, don't you agree? We are, after all, human beings placed on earth to live our lives to the fullest and to respect the lives of others."

View of Carcross from the railway bridge. Note the size of tree Johnnie had to drive over to hit the Caribou

He didn't dress for success. A potential customer meeting Johnnie for the first time might pass over the grizzled man with his trademark cowboy hat, leather beaded jacket, and old clothes – seeking someone who looked more like a prosperous hunter who hosted the world elite should. They soon learned that in Johnnie's case, clothes didn't make the man but they did reflect who he was.

His wardrobe was what someone who lived on the land and off the land should wear. Johnnie was comfortable with himself and if his clothes were an issue for some people, that was their problem – not his.

"Life and nature have their own special magic," he told a very young Hollie Smith in the 1950s. "When you think about it, being able to see beyond the surface and understand something is kind of magical because not many people are able to do that...Most people go around wearing blinders and only see something if it's obvious. Often they only see what they want to see but by using your mind, coupled with observation, you can figure out almost anything."

He was uneducated – in the formal sense of the word. He only finished grade four in the school system but understood the value of knowledge and believed in sharing what he knew. His book learning may have been limited but his understanding of the land and of the underlying nature of people was beyond measure for those willing to sit and talk with him.

His clients were the highly educated, well-travelled of the world's rich and famous. They journeyed for weeks over thousands of miles by trains and ship not just to hunt with him but to share hours of conversation around the campfire at night. Their trips into the wilderness lasted anywhere from 30 to 65 days. They were intrigued by this individual who taught them how men and animals fit into the land and lived their lives in response to it as though the land itself was alive. They kept coming back.

"When you travel together," said Johnnie, "they (his clients) are like a part of you. You learn from them and they learn from you.

"I treated my hunters on the rough side and they liked it. I didn't wait on them. In fact, sometimes they waited on me. My hunters were big shots from Europe and the States. But I took them out and made men of them. I have friends all over the world. I could go anywhere and have a place to stay."

His regular clientele included military leaders, European royalty, business leaders (New York jeweller William Barthman, Chicago real estate developer Walter Buchen), politicians, writers (George Witter, author of A Funny Thing Happened... and A Hunt in the Yukon, Erle Stanley Gardner, the creator of Perry Mason both in print and on-screen), movie stars, artists (James Clark, the adventurer-artist who created wildlife sculptures for the American Museum of Natural History in New York), bankers, men and women alike – a Who's Who of people who would be a part of shaping the world during and after the Second World War.

Museums from around the world booked hunting trips with Johnnie so they could acquire world-class specimens of northern animal species to be preserved by a taxidermist for display in their natural history exhibits.

And there were the "interesting" guests. A well-known Chicago bootlegger in 1925 and, in 1935, Germany's Count Uxkull.

"This gentleman count," recalled Johnnie in 1987, "he tried to kill Hitler just before the end of the war. He placed a bomb under the table, but the table blocked the blast. They shot them all.

"He told me back (then) he expected trouble. He didn't like what was going on. Of course, when he tried to bomb Hitler and failed, they shot him."

Uxkull didn't physically try to blow up Adolf Hitler himself – his nephew Claus von Stauffenberg carried the bomb into the bunker – but the count was a leader in the plot and was hanged for his part in the assassination attempt. While awaiting word about whether or not the explosion had killed "der Fuhrer" on July 20, 1944, Uxkull entertained von Stauffenberg's children with stories about big game hunting.

It wasn't just hunters with guns who flocked to hunt with the man that many, including the Boone and Crockett Club, considered one of the top 10 guides in the world. The world's greatest bowman, archery equipment inventor, and manufacturer, Howard Hill was another frequent client. He was famous for making the iconic shot in the 1938 Errol Flynn film The Adventures of Robin Hood that split a target-embedded arrow in half.

Johnnie and his wilderness seduced them all.

American writer and industrialist John Batten of Racine, Wisconsin spent sixty-five days isolated from the world in the mountains of the eastern Yukon. He wrote that as he was boarding the train for the trip back to "civilization": "I waved a last goodbye to Johnnie Johns and for the first time in two months felt very lonely indeed."

When Walter Buchan found out he was dying one of the last things he wanted to do in life was go on a final hunt with his friend.

"Johnnie," he wrote in a letter, "I guess my hunting days are over. I have a bad heart. I think I've got one hunt left though, and I'm going to have it with you." He died a month before the planned hunt.

Being under a tree played a significant role throughout Johnnie's life.

When asked in 1959 by England's Queen Elizabeth II where he had been born, Johnnie replied, "I was born under a Spruce tree ma'am, at the south end of Tagish Lake. There were no hospitals in those days."

Being an outfitter hadn't been Johnnie's original goal in life.

"My father was teaching me trapping and hunting," Johnnie said in 1973, "then along came the mission school…. We didn't have professional teachers, just missionaries."

The missionaries pushed him to become a priest but there were other priorities. He was the bread earner for his family from the age of 13 after his father was injured in an accident. Forced to leave school and too young to work for the railroad he supported his family off the land by hunting, trapping, and fishing, then selling the meat and furs.

One fall day in 1916 he sat down to rest under a tree, worn out after a day of packing meat out of the bush. There was an old weathered magazine lying on the ground which he picked up to read. Barely visible on the front cover was the magazine's name, Outdoor Life, and on the back cover were some faded ads – one of which promoted an outfitter and read: "Hire Yourself a Guide."

"My God," he said to himself, "I could do that!"

Johnnie followed up by getting himself commissioned as a hunting guide in 1917 then, for $2.50, purchased an ad in Outdoor Life the next year and set up his own business. His first client was a remittance man, Alan Smith, from Philadelphia.

"They paid him to stay away from home," said Johnnie, "so he fished and hunted." Alan was also well known and respected in international hunting circles. One successful hunt with Alan and no further advertising was necessary. The remittance man talked up his experience, convincing others to book a hunt with Johnnie.

"I didn't know I was any good. People told me that.... I always wanted to succeed in what I was doing. When I started I didn't know one end of a horse from the other. But I watched people and learned from them.... I took out as many as 17 hunters at a time. I was making $100 per day, per hunter (in the 1930s, $150 per month was considered a living wage in the United States). It wasn't all gravy though. I hired one guide for each hunter and had to feed the horses."

With the exception of the railroad, which accounted for almost 80% of employment in Carcross, Johnnie was the single biggest employer and largest industry in Carcross in the 1920s and '30s. His outfitting business was one of the largest in the world.

His clients filled the Caribou, its restaurant and bar for most of the summer and fall every year. He purchased every product and service he could from the local merchants thus ensuring their survival at a time when small business across North America was starting to wither. High unemployment and unequal wealth distribution characterized the "Roaring '20s" and the Great Depression in the 1930s.

Even though they knew they had an advantage local businessmen needed to be on their toes when doing business with Johnnie. When he decided to purchase a car from Dawson City resident Clarence Craig in 1933 he negotiated a trade: $10 cash and four marten skins rather than the $50 cash that Clarence was asking. Furriers, he told Clarence, would pay $10 each for the pelts in Vancouver so neither man was going to lose anything in this deal.

When Clarence went to sell the skins in Vancouver they fetched only two dollars each. He simply shook his head, laughed at himself for being so gullible and the two men remained friends for the rest of their lives. Johnnie was a hard man to dislike or hold a grudge against.

He earned a fortune but gave much of his money to friends and family in need. Whenever a community event needed financial support, Johnnie was there to help.

"You'd starve to death if you had nothing but money.... It was the life I liked and I made it pay. I worked and played at the same time."

Although his advertising brochure warned, "We do not furnish women or liquor...bring your own," he guaranteed his clients good food, good trophies and, above all, a good time.

He wasn't averse to joining his clients to "do the town" when their hunt was over. In Carcross, that meant spending the night partying in the Caribou. Sometimes they would barhop over to the Scott Hotel but after that burned down in 1936 the number of drinking holes in town was rather limited. Shutting down the place (drinking until closing time and beyond if possible) wasn't in the brochure but it was definitely part of the good-time guarantee.

Johnnie recited poetry or regaled his guests with stories of other hunts: fishing stories, facing down charging Grizzly bears, nose-to-nose encounters with moose, or trips where his hunters were affected by "buck fever" and couldn't pull the trigger after getting a sheep or caribou in their rifle sights. All the while the booze, especially Black Velvet Canadian rye whiskey, flowed freely.

When Johnnie told a story he didn't just tell the story. He acted out all the parts — flapping his arms when a bird, holding his hands up as antlers while being a caribou or stalking his prey between the tables as the hunter.

John Batten didn't remember much of the evening of drinking before his cousins, John and Alice Pirie, were due to leave after their hunt. However, he did write about waking up in the middle of the night with the urge to satisfy the inevitable result of drinking too much before going to bed. Still partially inebriated and not quite awake he mistakenly thought the curtains of his second-floor room in the Caribou looked like the flaps of the tent he had been living in for the past month.

When he tried to walk out of "the tent" he banged his shin on the windowsill and his head on the sash of the open sliding window. His cousins, hearing a dreadful racket from his room, came in to rescue him before he could try again and steered him out of the room into the hall toward the communal toilet.

One evening after celebrating another successful hunt Johnnie's daughter Ada received a call at home from her father, telling her he had had an accident — he had run into the Caribou with his truck.

Thinking he had hit "a" caribou, Ada asked him if he had saved the hide. It took a number of tries before she understood he had driven his truck over a tree planted beside the hotel and into the side of "the" Caribou and there was no hide to save. There was no safe place to hide either.

Unveiling of the 2015 Canada Post stamp issued in Bessie's honor

Chapter 15

SPIRITED AWAY IN THE NIGHT

A hotel will have hundreds, possibly thousands of customers sleeping in its beds in a year. Enough guests that inevitably some of those customers check out before they check-out.

Hotels usually like to keep those kinds of details under wraps. The deceased are usually removed from the hotel in late mornings when there are few customers around to witness their departure, preferably through a door where there's nobody around at all. It's not something staff are encouraged to talk about.

"Yes, we have a room that became available unexpectedly this morning. Mr. Smith was supposed to leave on Tuesday but he died last night. It's very quiet and overlooks the back parking lot. What time will be you be arriving?"

Of course, that reticence to chat about who died in your hotel can disappear when there's a ghost involved. There is such a public fascination with ghosts that instead of being hidden it becomes a selling feature – spend the night in a haunted hotel!!

It's like an ethereal presence can convince a customer that someone really didn't die in the same bed they are currently occupying – the body may have stopped functioning but their soul lives on and it is that inexplicable possibility that has grasped the public imagination.

When you do rent the room you're not likely to be disturbed by an apparition. They're not employees and don't work according to the local labour code. Paying a little extra to spend the night in a haunted space doesn't guarantee you will see, feel or hear anything at all. None of that seems to matter to true believers or sometimes, even the skeptics.

Independent polls taken in 2005 and 2006 showed that one in three people believe in the possibility of ghosts. One in five reported they have seen or encountered a ghost at some point in their lives. There are approximately 6,000 haunted hotels, houses, churches, office buildings, and other commercial attractions operating as commercial attractions in the United States. There are probably plenty more that aren't being publicized or capitalized on as a business.

Of those who indicated they didn't believe or weren't sure if they believed in ghosts, many also added the caveat that they were still scared of them.

Science has tried to explain hauntings as the imaginative products of a creative mind, the paranoia of a fearful mind, misinterpreted noises, waking dreams, suggestibility, schizophrenia or the possibility of hallucinations brought on by toxic substances, alcohol or drugs. One study suggested that people who experience ghostly events are usually people who believe they will have such an encounter before it occurs and take note of the conditions that confirm their expectations.

Some historians refuse to put a ghost or a haunting in their writings. "They don't exist, therefore they're not part of the history," they insist.

Another school of thought suggests hauntings are our way of filling gaps in the verifiable historical record because paranormal tales are usually rooted in unsubstantiated stories or legends. Even if we don't believe in the paranormal there is still uncertainty. We tell the tale of ghosts rather than risk discovering spirits actually exist.

In other words, even though they may not be a part of the physical, substantiated history they are still a part of the story and deserve to be treated as such.

Hotel staircase was the only access to the top floors

In an older building like the Caribou there are cold spots, creaking sounds, and odd noises that might be mistaken as footfalls and explained by science. Then there are the stories for which there are no explanations – told by people who had no prior knowledge of the Caribou's otherworldly residents and no expectations at all.

Bessie is the oldest historical manifestation in the Caribou but she is not alone. There is another who turned up shortly after her.

At some time in the mid-1930s a trapper damaged his leg while working near his cabin and was unable to walk. He dragged himself into the cabin so he wouldn't freeze to death outside. However, he only had a limited amount of wood to stoke his stove and no way to haul more in. Once the fuel ran out the killing cold would gradually seep permanently into the log walls, his bed, and finally, into him.

There was no way to communicate with the outside world – some trappers did have radios but they were expensive and most couldn't afford them. He didn't have the medical knowledge to repair the damage, but even fixing it up would only keep him alive long enough to freeze to death.

Barely able to pull himself around the small cabin to eat and drink he became increasingly dehydrated and starved, eventually unable to get out of bed at all.

Many trapper's cabins are set up so the occupant can feed wood into the stove without getting out of bed. It's a convenience that allows the individual to start a fire and heat up the interior of the cabin each morning without getting out from under their warm covers into the morning chill.

He was feeding his final few sticks into the flames, knowing the inevitable was creeping closer, when another trapper pulled up with his dog team in front of the cabin for an unexpected visit with his closest neighbour.

The injured trapper was in pretty rough shape when he arrived in Carcross and they put him into a third-floor room in the Caribou while they waited for the doctor to arrive from Whitehorse. Despite all their efforts his time ran out and he died there.

When they quietly spirited his body away some part of him decided it liked the place and stayed.

He still limps around the third floor at night. Hotel guests have reported hearing him although no one has ever actually reported seeing him although it is possible that Dorothy Hopcott may have encountered him when she owned the hotel in the 1960s.

Chapter 16

PRELUDE
TO
WAR

Less than a month after Bessie's death her sister and sole beneficiary of her will, Louise Dawson, arrived from California to take over operation of the hotel. Her son Harold Corby, his wife Grace, and two grandchildren, Donald and Caroline, accompanied her.

Unbeknownst to Louise, Bessie hadn't been able to meet the lease payments since Edwin's death. Not wanting to take over the hotel herself, Annie Auston had allowed Bessie to stay there anyway. She extended the same courtesy to Louise.

According to travelling salesman John Rowland who stayed in the Caribou in 1937, Louise was "a delightful person.... The Caribou Hotel was first class in all respects, good food prepared by the expert hand of Louise Dawson, clean pleasant rooms with a view. It was a far cry from some of the hotels where I stayed when I didn't know whether to sweep out my room or plow it.

"I was reluctant to leave the beautiful spot even though I had finished all my calls, so decided to stay over an extra day."

The Dawsons and Corbys managed the hotel until 1938 when they terminated their lease with Annie Auston. They moved across the street to where they had built another hotel, the Carcross Inn, a one-and-a-half storey building with six rooms.

Other than the Caribou itself, the Carcross Inn had no other competition in town. The Scott Hotel had burned down in 1936 but by then it wasn't really being used as a hotel anyway. The local school was located on its main floor and the former bar area was being used as a teahouse and lecture room for Patsy Henderson to tell his story of the discovery of Klondike gold to the tourists.

Ownership of the Caribou reverted to Annie but she just shut it down. When she passed away a few months later the hotel was inherited by her adopted son Bobbie.

When Annie and Arthur married they were too old to have children but Arthur wanted desperately to raise one. Both of Annie's children with Dawson Charlie had died shortly after his death in 1909.

One of Arthur's former police colleagues, Tom Dickson, had also married a native woman, Louise George. They had 13 children. The Dicksons agreed to allow the Austons to legally adopt one of their children — Bobbie.

When he inherited the Caribou Bobbie and his wife Dora were living and working in Pennington — a WPYR section camp a few miles south of Carcross on Bennett Lake.

Polly had been moved across the street to the Carcross Inn temporarily during the closure. He returned to the Caribou in late 1938 when Bobbie and Dora moved into the hotel and reopened it.

Their oldest daughter Annie — named after her grandmother — was still crawling when they took over the hotel.

The hotel was busy. "There were lots of people always coming and going," said Annie. Dora spent most of her time in the kitchen. Bobbie worked endless hours in and around the building and babysitting chores fell to their friend Tommy Brooks who apparently was easily distracted.

"My dad told me that the people in the bar would put their drinks on the floor with just a small mouthful of beer in them and I would crawl around the bar floor, tipping the glasses and drinking from them," Annie remembered in 2018. "He told me, 'If we didn't know where you were, we could find you in the bar.' I didn't drink as an adult and I still don't today. 'That's why you don't like drinking now,' he would tell me when he was an elder, 'because you used to enjoy it too much when you were a baby.'"

The Austons also discovered one of the more disruptive issues about owning a bar and living in the hotel. Despite the fact that selling booze after-hours was illegal, throughout the night and into the early mornings people would hammer on the front door, directly below the suite where they slept, and demand to be sold their favorite – a quart bottle of Pilsener beer with an eight percent alcohol content..

"Bobbie! Wake up!" they shouted and eventually Polly would join in the cacophony, "Bobbie! Wake up! Bobbie Wake up!" It was a problem that was never going to go away. It got even worse for future managers and owners after 1969 when alcohol off-sales in the Yukon were expanded to 24-hours a day and the drinking age was lowered from 21 to 19 years of age.

The Second War must have come as a bit of relief for them after a year of hard work and interrupted sleep. Bobbie enlisted in the Canadian Army in 1939. He saw action in Operation Husky, the invasion and campaign to liberate Sicily in 1943.

With Bobbie leaving for an indeterminate period of time, he and Dora leased the hotel to Jack and Adele McMurphy in late 1939.

U.S. Army Air Corps Brigadier General William 'Billy' Mitchell cautioned that Alaska was strategically vital to North American defence

Chapter 17

THE
WAR
COMES
NORTH

"Alaska is the keystone of the Pacific arch...," US Army General William "Billy" Mitchell told a Congressional hearing in Washington, DC, 1935. "Japan is our dangerous enemy in the Pacific. They won't attack Panama. They will come right here to Alaska.... I believe in the future, he who holds Alaska will hold the world, and I think it is the most important strategic place in the world."

He was ignored by the politicians who may have agreed with his thinking but didn't care. The US wasn't at war with Japan; the pending conflagration in Europe was Europe's problem; there was the Depression to deal with; and, there was still an anti-war hangover from their involvement in the Great War.

Not until 1940 did they start to pay attention to the US's northern territory. A rumour, which later proved to be false, that Russia and Germany were building a military base on Big Diomede Island in the Bering Strait — the body of water that separates Russia from Alaska — sparked fears that Alaska could possibly be a target for belligerent forces.

Congress voted for a record defence budget for Alaska that year. Air bases were to be built at Anchorage, Kodiak, Yakutat, and on Annette Island in the panhandle part of the territory. A naval base was to be built at Dutch Harbor in the Aleutian Islands.

Military personnel in Alaska were bolstered and a string of emergency landing fields were constructed stretching from Nome on Norton Sound to Northway, close to the Canadian border.

On the Canadian side of the border a series of airfields running from Edmonton, Alberta, to Whitehorse, Yukon, had been authorized when Canada declared war on Germany in 1939. The purpose was to provide an aerial highway along which troops and supplies could be rapidly deployed in the event of an emergency but no construction had actually yet been done. The northwest corner of Canada wasn't high on the priority list of a military focused on the fighting in Europe.

A Canadian-American Permanent Joint Board on Defence was set up in August, 1940, and work on the airstrips was started in 1941. Eight additional aerodromes were added northwest of Whitehorse reaching as far as Snag – a weather station in the middle of nowhere but just a short hop across the border from Northway, Alaska.

America's Lend-Lease program with Russia sent over 8,000 aircraft between 1942 and 1945 along what became known as the Northwest Staging Route, which used both the Canadian and American landing strips. The planes were flown from Montana into Alberta, then north through northern BC, the Yukon, and across Alaska to Nome where Russian pilots would take over to ferry the aircraft into Siberia and ultimately to the Russian front against Germany.

There had been many dreams of building an overland route to Alaska. In 1904, US railway builder, F.H. Harriman, had proposed a railroad that would not only link Alaska to the lower 48 but also Russia through a tunnel or bridge under or across the Bering Strait.

Canada's Northwest Mounted Police actually started building a highway in 1905 and completed just over 600 kilometres of road north of Fort Saint John before the project was cancelled.

Another proposal in 1928 made a road to Alaska part of a grander scheme to link Panama with the Polar Sea.

U.S. Army troops in Skagway boarding a White Pass train destined for Carcross and Whitehorse

In 1933, a joint Canada-US commission was struck to study the feasibility of a highway to Alaska, but did no work for the first five years of its mandate.

When the guns started firing in Europe with Germany's invasion of Poland in September, 1939, the joint commission did come up with some possible routes.

Route A, preferred by the Americans, started in Prince George, BC, went up to Whitehorse, Yukon then to Fairbanks, Alaska.

Route B, which the Canadians liked, also started in Prince George but was further east than Route A, missing Whitehorse before swinging west through Dawson City, Yukon to Fairbanks.

Arctic explorer Vilhjalmur Stefansson suggested a route from Edmonton that paralleled the Mackenzie River north before heading west to Fairbanks.

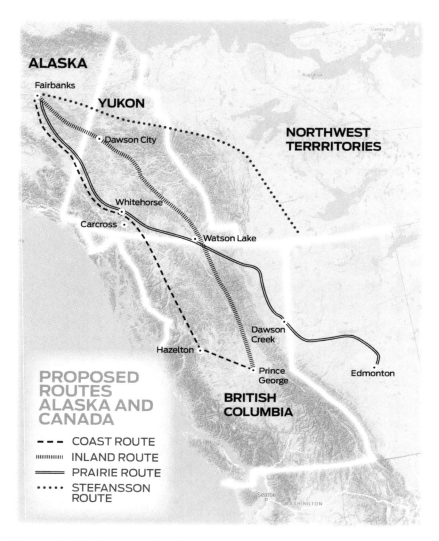

ALASKA
Fairbanks
YUKON
Dawson City
NORTHWEST
TERRRITORIES
Whitehorse
Carcross
Watson Lake
Dawson
Creek
Hazelton
Prince
George
Edmonton
BRITISH
COLUMBIA

PROPOSED
ROUTES
ALASKA AND
CANADA

- - - COAST ROUTE
IIIIIIII INLAND ROUTE
═══ PRAIRIE ROUTE
····· STEFANSSON
ROUTE

The route finally determined to be the most practical used an existing highway from Edmonton to Dawson Creek, BC. From Dawson Creek, which also had a rail link to southern BC, they would head north through Fort St. John, Fort Nelson to Watson Lake, Whitehorse and Carcross in the Yukon, to Delta Junction just southeast of Fairbanks.

It was far enough inland to avoid attacks from enemy aircraft; they could use the WPYR to move equipment and men to Whitehorse and Carcross; and, it linked the proposed airfields.

Military train crossing trestle on the White Pass and Yukon Route

It would cost $25 million to build and would take four to five years to complete, but there was no rush and no real need. It was just a plan in case something happened – which it probably wouldn't.

Japan bombing Pearl Harbour on Dec. 7, 1941, changed everything.

Suddenly the west coast of North America, including Alaska, was considered vulnerable to a possible Japanese invasion. Billy Mitchell's almost forgotten warning about the strategic value of Alaska had renewed significance.

A special cabinet committee was struck by US President Franklin Roosevelt to determine how quickly a road could be built to Alaska. The Canadian government furnished a right of way, gave permission to harvest timber, gravel, and rock along the proposed route, waived import duties, income and sales taxes, and suspended immigration regulations for American troops and contractors who would be spending most of their time working in Canada. The Americans agreed to pay for the construction and to hand the highway over to Canada six months after the cessation of hostilities.

The 2,200-kilometre highway, called the Alcan (ALaska CANada), was going to be a simple track through the bush. It only had to be good enough for military convoys to travel on and much of it would have to be engineered even as it was being built. Money was no obstacle: it would cost what it would cost, and it had to be finished as soon as possible – in months, not years.

On Feb. 2, 1942, the order was given to start work and 11,000 soldiers, along with civilian contractors, were mobilized. A month later, the first troops arrived in Dawson Creek.

It wasn't until the middle of April that men and equipment were transported by ships up the west coast from Seattle, Washington to Skagway, Alaska.

In 1942, Skagway was largely a ghost town with only about 450 permanent residents. Other than some summer tourism and the WPYR there was little happening in the small harbour settlement.

Mostly, it consisted of derelict buildings – brothels, hotels, and saloons constructed for the stampeders heading to the gold fields of the Klondike at the end of the nineteenth century.

The US Army set up a pup tent city on the airfield, clogged the streets with their equipment then went to check out the tracks.

The railroad had been built for light trains that one engine could pull up the impossibly steep grades from Skagway once or twice a day. The Alcan campaign would demand trains so heavy that three engines were required to pull and a fourth to push each one over the mountains up to 35 times a day. Long stretches of rails and ties had to be replaced. Bridges as well as portions of the rail bed needed to be reinforced or completely rebuilt.

The Army wasn't interested in upgrading the railroad – work on the highway needed to commence as quickly as possible. They commandeered the railroad for the duration of the war, purchased additional train engines, and pressed retired rolling stock back into service. They manufactured railcars designed to carry their bulldozers, scrappers, graders, dump trucks, generators, and welding machines. When rails split or the rail bed slumped they repaired as required but for the moment speed was of the essence.

In early April the US Army started to trickle into Carcross.

White Pass train in Skagway loaded with equipment for building the Alcan Highway

Black troops detrain at Carcross train station

Chapter 18

"BLACK WHITE MEN"

For seven-year-old Millie McMurphy the Caribou was just like a big playhouse.

Upstairs, her parents converted one of the rooms, on the third floor overlooking the WPYR train station, into a playroom for her.

Downstairs was Polly and helping her mother in the restaurant, which she considered to be fun rather than work. When helping in the restaurant she could listen to the tales of the cat skinners who hauled freight to and from Atlin in winter, the passengers off the Tutshi fresh from their time at Ben-My-Chree in summer, and from the train who stopped to have lunch before continuing their journey, and Johnnie Johns.

Connecting the two was the staircase with long banisters down which she loved to slide. When showing people around the hotel almost 80 years later Millie handed off her cane and jumped onto the banister leading down from the third floor. "Don't worry. I've done this a thousand times," she said as she descended rapidly toward the second floor.

Her father, Jack, was the station agent for the WPYR in Carcross in 1939. He had arrived into the north two decades earlier to work on the telegraph line between Carcross and Conrad City. During one visit to Carcross he met Adele, who was from Whitehorse and had just taken a teaching position in Carcross. At the time, the school was located in an old garage and the teacher lived in the school. There was also a classroom located in the Scott Hotel.

Jack decided he wanted to marry Adele so he quit his job and walked out of the bush into town. For several years he drove a dog team for Ross Hebert, doing the mail run between Carcross and Atlin but, in 1932, Northern Airways took over the postal contract and dog team mail delivery ended so Jack took a job with the WPYR.

Adele left teaching to take over management of the hotel when they decided to lease it from Bobbie Auston. A few months later, on Sept. 1, 1939, Germany invaded Poland and war began.

Carcross felt the impact almost immediately. Johnnie Johns's business dropped off as hunts were cancelled and future bookings went unfilled. Many of his clients were directly involved in one aspect or another of the conflict.

The rooms in the Caribou, usually fully booked in the hunting months, went empty. There was no rationing in the Yukon but some foodstuffs were hard to come by and the restaurant menu started to look pretty thin and subject to last-minute changes. An order of pork might be received as beef instead. The explanation often heard from the shipping company was "it started out as pork when it left but it was beef when it got here".

Alcohol sales and Jack's income from his day job kept the business afloat for the next two years.

Other than knowing their meagre existence was probably going to be a little more meagre until the fighting ended the residents of Carcross were generally not much concerned about the war and knew nothing of what the US Army had planned for them. At least, not until the first American troops unexpectedly started arriving in early April, 1942, and the US Army imposed an eight percent war tax on all goods sold in the town.

Once Carcrossians realized their little community was going to be a marshalling point in a major war effort they made one concession. They hung blackout curtains over their windows in the event of an air raid by the Japanese.

Although the US Army identified the Caribou as a central part of their staging area in Carcross they never commandeered the hotel. Other than the officers and soldiers who arrived early in April, 1942, few military men actually stayed in the hotel. The early arrivals weren't there to build the highway. Even though the Army wasn't taking over the hotel, their job was to make improvements to the accommodations for civilian contractors, install plumbing, and convert the bottom floor into a mess hall. Once that was complete they were to locate a suitable site for their camp.

The Army put in new washrooms with chemical toilets on each floor and made sure there was a washstand with a basin and water jug in each room. A communal bathtub was installed on the second floor and a communal shower on the third. A system for providing them with running water was put in, pulling water directly from Bennett Lake and emptying the dirty water back into the lake – which worked fine in the summer months but was ineffectual in the winter when the lake was frozen.

The dining room was divided into two parts. A small dining area at the front of the hotel, with all the windows, with the main eating area behind it with no windows at all. The kitchen was left where it always was at the back of the hotel. Because the demand on the kitchen was going to substantially increase they switched out the old wood cooking stove for a propane one.

For the next three years the Caribou was the dining room for some of the military brass and home to civilian contractors who worked for Hatfield Electric, Betchel Price and Callahan Constructors (BPC), and Marwell Construction.

In Skagway, the American commander, General William Hoge, decided the 340th regiment would spearhead the road building to the south from a camp at Tagish – close to the site of the village the Indigenous population of Carcross originally occupied. However, to get the 340th to Tagish, a road had to be built south from Carcross. He ordered the 93rd Engineer Battalion to proceed to Carcross and construct the route that would take the 340th to their base.

Millie, her two sisters, and everyone else in Carcross were about to get an insight into what life was like for a black person in the deep south of the United States in the 1940s. The 93rd was one of three black regiments assigned to the Alcan project.

Word spread that the next train to arrive in Carcross on May 1, 1942, would be loaded with "coloured" troops. The entire student body, all 14 of them including Millie, rushed out of school before being dismissed for the day. None of them had ever seen a black man before. Breathless with excitement they raced to the train depot and watched as the "black white men" stepped off the train.

The US Army hadn't even wanted non-white soldiers when they recognized the looming probability of being eventually drawn into the European war and started recruiting in 1940. President Franklin Roosevelt stated he had no political will to deal with civil rights and Army Chief of Staff George Marshal wrote that racism in the United States wasn't the military's problem and they shouldn't be required to make any effort to resolve it.

Despite the political and bureaucratic efforts to block the enlistment of black soldiers, it did occur. However, the American government determined that there would be few, if any, black officers in the corps because as US Secretary of War Henry Stimson wrote, "...leadership was not embedded in the negro race yet."

In December, 1940, white officers were assigned to take command of a regiment consisting of black non-commissioned officers and enlisted men who were activated in February, 1941, as the 93rd Engineer Battalion.

Putting on a uniform did bring some benefits for a black man that remaining a civilian in the United States possibly wouldn't have. They were paid a regular wage — apparently the same as the white soldiers. They received specialized training and skills — truck driving, cat skinning, office administration, vehicle mechanics, welding, etc. — that might have been denied them had they not enlisted and would have practical application when their stint in the army ended.

However, despite the fact they were isolated and almost as far away from the southern states as one could get without leaving the continent they were, in the eyes of some white Americans, still "niggers" and the "separate but equal " racism that label came with was still there.

It wasn't as if Canada and Carcross didn't have their own versions of racism — the Indian Act, Bishop Bompas dictating that "natives" live on the south side of the narrows with everyone else on the north, and the Chout'la Residential School for native children — but it was a different form of legislated bigotry from that which existed in the US.

Soldiers singing and dancing on the train platform while waiting to move out to their encampment

Canada legislated assimilation of the indigenous culture into the dominant European society. US legislation was based upon segregation – the separation of cultures with a hierarchy based solely upon skin color, with whites at the top and blacks on the bottom.

The cruelest part of Canadian law required that Indigenous children be separated from their parents and be taken to residential schools at a specified age in an attempt to isolate and educate them away from their cultural roots. The emotional, psychological, and sexual abuse those children endured was hidden for decades behind a conspiracy of silence founded on fear and distrust of white authority. The damage it ultimately did to Indigenous people was incalculable.

The Indian Act denied significant legal privileges to aboriginal people including the right of citizenship. The land's first peoples were not permitted to be citizens of their own country until 1961. Violations of the restrictions in the Indian Act were punishable by short jail sentences and fines.

However, there was no legal statute that dictated whether or not Indigenous people could walk in the streets, shop in stores or eat in restaurants alongside the Non-Indigenous population.

While unauthorized segregation happened in other parts of the country, in Carcross there was little unofficial apartheid. Indigenous people were part of the community as a whole.

US legislation was based on the principle of segregation – the separation and suppressing cultures based solely on skin color. In many US states, Jim Crow laws dictated where black Americans could eat, drink, learn, travel, sleep, walk, relax, work, who they could talk to, even where they could have a bowel movement. Failure to adhere to the law, whether the violation was real or simply perceived, was officially punished by fines or imprisonment and unofficially, by beatings and lynchings. The white perpetrators of the unofficial punishment, on the rare occasions they were arrested and charged with a crime, were leniently treated by the judicial system.

Other American jurisdictions didn't have the laws but systemic prejudice existed in principle although to a lesser extent. The Army recognized the Jim Crow rules and added a few of their own.

Black soldiers weren't allowed to associate with civilians nor socialize with locals. When they were in locations like Skagway where there weren't any segregated facilities they were allowed limited use of the local amenities but only as a group and under military police escort.

However, Skagway was a small town overwhelmed by thousands of soldiers and intermingling between races, civilians and military personnel was inevitable. One of the reasons General Hoge sent the 93rd north was to quickly get them out of town and avoid any potential problems. Carcross, he must have thought, was secluded enough that any issues could be dealt with quietly. The soldiers would mostly be out of town working on the road so the possibility of any concerns arising was remote.

The black troops didn't like winter

The Army set up their camp near the airfield, almost two kilometres out of Carcross, hoping the distance would be sufficient to keep the soldiers and locals separated.

The residents of Carcross didn't understand the concept of segregation.

Adele McMurphy wasn't surprised that black soldiers walked into town and came to the hotel. She was startled when they knocked on the back door instead of coming through the front like everyone else and astonished when informed that the Caribou was off limits. Whites could go in but black soldiers weren't allowed to enter. They could sit on her back porch but that was as far as they could go.

The concept of restricting access because of skin colour had never occurred to her.

Initially, all they were looking for was a drink of water but the aroma of fresh-baked bread from her oven and discovering she made her own ice cream captured their attention. The Army mess tent had a limited fare – chilli, beef hash, and vegetable hash – and it was of dubious quality. They kept coming back.

When one of the black soldiers noticed there was a piano in the hotel he mentioned he knew how to play it. Adele had it rolled out onto the back porch and the man started playing Al Dexter's future hit song "Pistol Packing Mama" (the March, 1942, recording by Al Dexter and his Troopers would hit number 2 on the US Juke Box Folk Records chart in 1943 – right behind Bing Crosby's version of the same song at number 1).

Impromptu concerts became a regular event on the Caribou porch with the piano accompanied by quartets singing or soldiers playing guitars and harmonicas they had brought with them. The locals gathered to listen, mingling with the musicians and soldiers.

Everything that was happening at the Caribou was a violation of Army regulations. Wisely, the white officers chose to ignore the rule breaking, possibly fearing a backlash, not from the soldiers but from the local population who were enjoying the entertainment and couldn't understand why the restrictions existed in the first place.

Millie had never heard anything like "Pistol Packing Mama" before and every time the music started she couldn't help but start to dance. One musical evening, while helping her mother in the restaurant and stepping lively at the same time, she spun to place a stack of clean plates on a table – and missed the table.

Some Yukon residents were uncomfortable with the black soldiers – not because they had any negative expectations of them but because they didn't know what to expect.

Dawson City resident Nancy Firth was traveling on the WPYR in a train filled with black soldiers on her way back home after a brief visit "outside". Like most northerners her experience with black people was limited. While her four-year-old daughter paraded up and down the railcar playing with, talking to, and laughing along with the solders she sat petrified in her seat not knowing how to cope with being a visible minority. It never occurred to her that she was experiencing the discomfort the same soldiers she was so frightened of lived with all of their lives – with none of the horrors of racism and hatred that often accompanied it.

First Nation guides guiding U.S. Army survey crew during construction of Alcan Highway

Chapter 19

BUILDING
THE
ALCAN

With his outfitting business effectively shut down for the duration of the war Johnnie Johns and another Carcross native, Billy Smith, made themselves available to the US Army. The Army took them up on their offer to help their surveyors find a route from Carcross to Tagish where the 340th would establish their base. From there they would continue until they hooked up with the route being blazed from the south. The army also rented horses from Johnnie.

Originally, the plan was to build a straight road then orders arrived to make it crooked so enemy aircraft couldn't effectively strafe convoys. The new orders suited Johnnie perfectly.

Knowing the war probably wouldn't last forever but the road would be around long after the military left Johnnie determined how to make this work to his advantage. He would mark out trails close to certain lakes so instead of having to walk through the bush to his favourite fishing holes he could drive there once peace came again.

The area they were going to build through was full of swamps and bogs.

When the lieutenant in charge of the road marking crew which Johnnie was going to guide showed up with tripods and rods for surveying, Johnnie told him to leave the equipment behind.

"It doesn't make sense," he told the officer, "because you are going to spend a lot of time cutting lines through the trees. Then you'll do your survey. Then you'll have to do it all over again because it doesn't account for the land.

"Build from Jackpine (tree) to Jackpine. Jackpine needs good solid land in which to grow." It was only coincidental that the Jackpine stands also happened to be near to the lakes Johnnie wanted access to.

When the crew headed off into the bush on May 6, 1942, they could hear the bulldozers behind them roaring into life and the crashing of men armed with saws, axes, and shovels starting to clear the way.

While there was wisdom in Johnnie's thinking there was madness in the execution of his plan as he led the US Army on a merry chase through the bush.

The bulldozers were literally right on their heels and they had to keep moving quickly to avoid being hit by trees getting knocked down. When Johnnie or the lieutenant reached a point where they couldn't see the machinery behind them, one of the trail blazing crew would find a tree and push on it to make it wave. The cat skinner behind them would spot the moving tree and head in that direction.

Their only relief came when the bulldozers started to run low on fuel. Gas and diesel had to be brought up the "truck trail" from the field of fuel drums behind the WPYR depot. The highway at this stage was a single one-way, deeply rutted, mud pit of a track just wide enough to give passage to a truck. Then it had to be hand pumped into the fuel tanks, which gave the crew Johnnie was guiding time to take a breather. Then the relentless chase would begin again.

On May 28 they reached Tagish. There the 93rd built a ferry, moved men and equipment across the Six-Mile River, and continued south.

Johnnie stayed ahead of the bulldozers until they hooked up to a road being constructed from the south by Teslin resident George Johnson. George had purchased a car and was building himself a five-kilometre road on which to drive it when the Alcan project began. His road eventually became a part of the highway.

The linking of the two meant Johnnie's contract with the Army was done. He went back to hunting, fishing, and spending days in the Caribou

U.S. Army bulldozer pushing the Alcan Highway into the northern wilderness

talking with Polly – telling stories and watching all the activity. Waiting for the war to come to an end so he could go back to work.

"They liked the country," said Johnnie in 1986, "The American soldiers did. The coloured people didn't like it so much. They were afraid of the bears in the woods. They wore woollen caps in summer because they were cold all the time."

Orders were sent out to move the 340th from Skagway to Tagish. They were tasked with upgrading the truck trail into a proper road. The few elements of the 93rd that remained in Carcross were sent north to where Army bulldozers continued to slash through the bush to Whitehorse.

Carcross was no longer a military operations base for the road construction but because of its proximity to the railroad remained a fuel and supply depot and motor pool for the American troops working both south toward Teslin and north toward Whitehorse.

U.S. Army camp for the 93rd Engineers at the base of Caribou Mountain near Carcross

On June 3, 1942, the Japanese finally launched the attack on North America's coast that many had feared. They bombed the American base at Dutch Harbor on Adak Island in Alaska's Aleutian chain. Two days later Japanese troops captured the nearby islands of Kiska and Attu, securing a foothold on American soil.

Chapter 20

THE CANADIAN OIL (CANOL) PROJECT

With the threat of further Japanese advances into Alaska, then down through Canada and into the US now front and centre in their thinking, the American military realized they needed a safe source of easily accessible fuel in the north. The only way to get diesel or gas to either Alaska or the Yukon was by tanker ship either up the Inside Passage to Skagway or across the open sea to Seward – routes which were both considered susceptible to attack.

Seventeen days after the occupation of Kiska and Attu a Japanese submarine torpedoed a ship off the coast of Washington, shelled a station on Vancouver Island, then fired on two naval stations in Oregon, validating their concerns about open sea routes to Alaska.

The Alcan was still six months from being able to handle heavy truck traffic.

There had been oil production in the Gulf of Alaska since 1911 but those oil fields were abandoned in 1933 when fire destroyed Alaska's only refinery at Katalla.

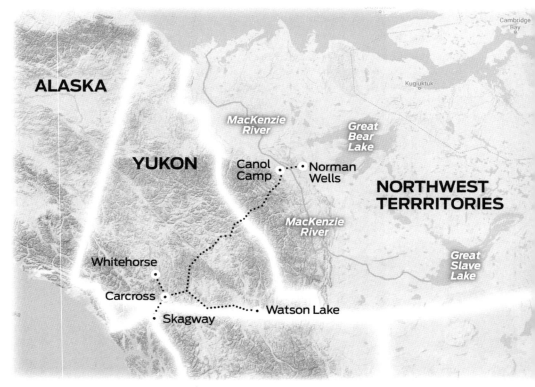

····· Canol Pipeline

The closest safe source of oil was a remote community called Norman Wells, located on the Mackenzie River in Canada's Northwest Territories. It had been producing a particularly suitable type of oil since 1920. The oil had low levels of paraffin in it and flowed easily in cold temperatures. There was even a small refinery in Norman Wells to meet the demands of the local population.

The Army proposed building a pipeline from Norman Wells to Whitehorse, Yukon – a distance of over 1,600 kilometres through uncharted wilderness, across a multitude of rivers, and over two mountain ranges. A refinery would be built in Whitehorse and fuel could be delivered up and down the Alcan Highway when it was completed. A secondary pipeline was also to be built to the coast, from Whitehorse through Carcross to Skagway, to send refined oil down for coastal shipping when the Japanese threat was mitigated.

Everything they would need to build the western portion of the pipeline could be delivered up the coast to Skagway and from there to Carcross on the railway. The risk of the building supplies coming under attack was there, they acknowledged, but there was no other way to do it.

From Carcross the pipeline materials would be trucked on the Alcan to Johnson's Crossing on the Teslin River, then up what came to be called the South Canol Road.

For the eastern portion being built from Norman Wells, everything would be barged down the Athabasca, Slave, and Mackenzie rivers from a base north of Edmonton, Alberta.

The attack on Dutch Harbor on June 3, 1942, woke the United States up to the danger of invasion by Japan and emphasized the need to find a northern fuel supply for American and Canadian forces

One of the barges making a delivery of Canol pipeline supplies to Norman Wells made a clandestine stop on Great Bear Lake during its return journey. There it picked up a load of a black ore called pitchblende – destined for the University of Chicago, which refined it into pure uranium 235 and sent it off to a top secret scheme called the Manhattan Project. The material delivered by the barge was used in the development of the atomic bombs dropped on Hiroshima and Nagasaki in August, 1945, bringing an end to the Second World War.

Caribou Hotel as the headquarters for contractors working on the Alcan highway and the Canol Pipeline

The pipeline was top secret – the public was already aware of the Alcan being built, but there was to be no mention of the Canol. Even the hiring poster for the civilian contractors made a point of not identifying the name of the project or the location of the job site although it was explicit about working conditions.

THIS IS NO PICNIC

WORKING AND LIVING CONDITIONS ON THIS JOB ARE AS DIFFICULT AS THOSE ENCOUNTERED ON ANY CONSTRUCTION JOB EVER DONE IN THE UNITED STATES OR FOREIGN TERRITORY. MEN HIRED FOR THIS JOB WILL BE REQUIRED TO WORK AND LIVE UNDER THE MOST EXTREME CONDITIONS IMAGINABLE. TEMPERATURES WILL RANGE FROM 90 DEGREES ABOVE ZERO TO 70 DEGREES BELOW ZERO. MEN WILL HAVE TO FIGHT SWAMPS, RIVERS, ICE AND COLD. MOSQUITOES, FLIES AND GNATS WILL NOT ONLY BE ANNOYING BUT WILL CAUSE BODILY HARM.

IF YOU ARE NOT PREPARED TO WORK UNDER THESE AND SIMILAR CONDITIONS DO NOT APPLY.

The Army was building the highway but the pipeline would mostly be constructed by civilian contractors under military direction. A consortium, BPC, was formed from three large US road and pipeline construction companies specifically for this project. Canada's Imperial Oil Company would develop the oil fields at Norman Wells. California's Standard Oil would build and operate the refinery in Whitehorse.

There was no budget. The pipeline, the road paralleling it, and the communication lines were to be built on a cost-plus basis and, like the highway, it would cost what it would cost. In the end it was the single largest and most expensive mega-project in world history to that time, officially costing the US government over $138 million (approximately $2.2 billion in 2018 dollars). Unofficial estimates place the actual cost at $300 million ($5.3 billion).

The Army, already running the WPYR at capacity to meet the needs of building the highway, added more trains to carry the pipes to Carcross plus pieces of a refinery dismantled in and shipped from Corpus Christi, Texas, destined for Whitehorse. Up to 35 trains a day rolled through the small town either en route to Whitehorse or unloading men, equipment, and pipes. Most of the pipe was then trucked to the Canol Road. Construction

Carcross as the equipment depot/maintenance yard for both the Alcan Highway and the Canol Pipeline

on the pipeline from Skagway to Whitehorse was started in October, 1942, and completed in January, 1943. Another pipeline was built from Carcross to Watson Lake, 500 kilometres to the southeast.

During the 20 months it took to build the entire Canol system, from Norman Wells to Watson Lake, Yukon to Skagway, Alaska to Carcross to Whitehorse, Yukon, over 25,000 men and women soldiers and civilians worked on the project.

Once again the rooms at the Caribou were full, this time with civilian contractors. Soldiers and contractors lined up in shifts for meals and the mess hall was packed. Having a full house and preparing three meals a day, seven days a week for dozens of diners must have exhausted Adele McMurphy because in 1943 she and Jack gave up their lease on the hotel. Dora Auston apparently didn't hire a new manager or find a new lessee – there was no need to. The US Army provided soldiers to supply housekeeping services and operate the Caribou restaurant until they pulled out in April, 1946. For the first time black soldiers were allowed into the hotel – but only as workers and they still had to use the back door.

Oil flowed from Normal Wells in December, 1943, and the refinery in Whitehorse started production in April, 1944, but the need for the pipeline was already past. The Japanese had been driven out of the Aleutians, the Alcan Highway was ready to handle heavy traffic like oil tankers, and the Allies were on the offensive everywhere in the Pacific. Eleven months after the refinery started up the US Army ordered it shut down.

When knowledge of the Canol project did become public late in 1942 it became a target for the Truman Committee, which had been set up to investigate waste and inefficiency in wartime contracts. The conclusion, published in early 1944, was that the project had been a colossal blunder by the US Army from beginning to end. The efficient manner in which the Canol investigation had been conducted by the committee was noticed by US President Franklin Roosevelt (FDR) who asked its chair, Missouri

Camp at Mile 173 of the Canol Pipeline

U.S. Army officers and contractors make a ceremonial weld on the Canol Pipeline

Senator Harry S. Truman, to be his running mate in the 1944 Presidential election. Truman became the 33rd President of the United States when FDR died on April 12, 1945.

The Army sold off the refinery in Whitehorse for a pittance of its original cost and then, in 1947, contracted out the dismantling of the pipeline as scrap metal. Ironically, the pipe was shipped out of the north by the identical route it originally traveled to get there. From the Canol Road and Watson Lake along the Alaska (formerly the Alcan) Highway to Carcross and on the WPYR to Skagway, then south down the coast.

Chapter 21

TOO
MANY
COOKS

One of the army mess sergeants came back to the Caribou around 1960.

Possibly because that might have been when he died. As to why he came back to the Caribou, who knows? Hundreds, possibly thousands of meals had been prepared in the hotel kitchen by military cooks in the final years of the war. No one has ever been able to identify which cook he was or what his attachment to the place is.

Perhaps the cook had been there earlier but nobody noticed. Not one owner or lessee mentioned his presence before the 1960s.

Bobbie Auston returned from the war just before the US Army and their civilian contractors withdrew from the highway and pipeline in 1946. The years apart had taken a toll on his marriage and he and Dora decided to separate. They closed the hotel and put it up for sale. It was allegedly offered to Johnnie Johns for $900 but he was busy rebuilding his outfitting business and turned down the opportunity. Polly temporarily moved across the street to the Carcross Inn again.

In either 1946 or 1947 Florence May Robson, known as May, purchased the Caribou but Bobbie always regretted letting go of the hotel. Even

Interior of Caribou Hotel restaurant as a mess hall for contractors working on the Alcan Highway and Canol Pipeline

though he went on to have a successful career as an outfitter and hunting guide he often remarked to his daughter, "Oh gosh Annie. I wish I hadn't sold that place."

If information about Bessie and Edwin Gideon before their Caribou Hotel days had been sparse, May Robson, or "ol' lady Robson" as the kids in Atlin used to call her, was even more of a historical mystery – apparently even to members of her own family.

"She was as prim and proper as you could make an older woman," said Willie Ross, who became her step-son when she married his father Bill in 1977, "But she was hard, strict, tough as nails and she never talked about anything. I thought she might have come from England because of her accent but she never talked about her past. I never even knew her maiden name (birth name)."

"She wore a dress and always had her hair in curlers. My father was sick when they got married – he had a hole in his chest they had made because he had cancer and when he smoked you could see the smoke curling up out of it. She was almost 80 years old and she nursed him until the day he died in 1979."

The only picture of May, taken in Atlin in about 1960, shows a solidly built, unsmiling woman.

Her obituary, published in the Chilliwack Progress in February, 1991, suggests she originally came from North Vancouver, BC, and lived in Whitehorse, Atlin, and Carcross before moving to Sardis, BC, where she died at the age of 92.

She had two children with the surname of Hall, which hints at a husband with that last name at some point in her life. In the list of those who survived and predeceased her there is no husband listed. May also apparently had another daughter with Bob Robson to whom Willie believed she was married when she purchased the Caribou but there is no mention of her in the list of family members.

Sixty days of rations for 1200 soldiers in Carcross

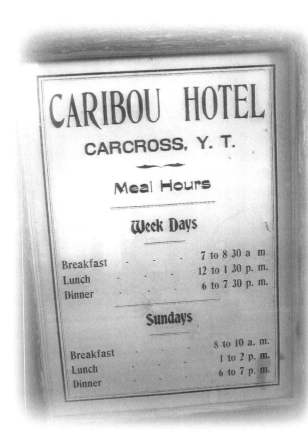

CARIBOU HOTEL

CARCROSS, Y. T.

Meal Hours

Week Days

Breakfast	· · ·	7 to 8 30 a m
Lunch	· · ·	12 to 1 30 p. m.
Dinner	· · ·	6 to 7 30 p. m.

Sundays

Breakfast	· · ·	8 to 10 a. m.
Lunch	· · ·	1 to 2 p. m.
Dinner	· · ·	6 to 7 p. m.

Wartime mess hall dining schedule found behind the restaurant wall in 2006

There are a lot of things a person will do in 90 years of living but no details are provided in the obituary with one noted exception – it specifically states she owned the Caribou Hotel in Carcross for nine years. Why the ownership of the hotel was important enough for the descendant who included that information while excluding everything else remains unknown.

There is no mention of the mess sergeant in her obituary.

Business at the Caribou was steady in the 1950s. The Royal Canadian Mounted Police didn't have a presence in the town during winter but they rented a room and rotated constables through the summer months. Johnnie Johns's outfitting business regained much of its former glory and once again provided a steady stream of well-heeled guests for the hunting season. The Yukon Exploration and Development Company had a major exploration venture ongoing in the Wheaton River Valley and their crews split accommodations between the Caribou and Carcross Inn. In winter, the WPYR housed train and maintenance crews in the Caribou. Train passengers still crowded the restaurant to visit with Polly.

However, some changes had diminished the importance of the community as a tourism destination and transportation hub.

The Alaska Highway was opened to public traffic in 1948 but rerouting in 1943 meant it now travelled a shorter path from Jake's Corner to Whitehorse, bypassing Carcross entirely.

In 1955, the WPYR permanently dry-docked the S.S. Tutshi and shut down their lodge at Ben-My-Chree because of declining business. The company had purchased the resort from the BC government, which took possession of the land after Otto and Kate Partridge died in 1930.

Cruise ship companies, which previously scheduled longer stopovers in Skagway to allow passengers to make an overnight trip on the railroad to Carcross, shortened their layover times and cut the inland excursions from their itineraries.

In 1948, Gladys and Alex MacKay leased the Caribou for one year. Every second weekend they hosted dances and a teenaged Millie McMurphy was one of the regular attendees. They didn't say anything about seeing an ethereal army cook.

A fire in 1939 destroyed the Chout'la Residential School but the war interrupted any plans to rebuild it until 1953 when Whitehorse builder Bob Warner was contracted to undertake the task. He leased the Caribou, turning it into a bunkhouse and dining hall for his construction crew until the job was completed near the end of 1954. There were no stories of phantom chef encounters during his stay.

Shortly after the school job was completed and Bob Warner terminated his lease, Mary Tobacco and June Fichner purchased the hotel from May Robson.

Mary was originally from Vancouver Island — a no-nonsense, baseball-loving beer-slinger who had worked for her aunt in a hotel in Nanaimo, BC before arriving in Carcross.

In the summers, she played ball during the day and tended bar in the evenings and nights. During winter, when the ball fields were covered with snow, she worked for the WPYR in addition to her duties at the hotel. Her winter wages helped keep the business afloat.

She may also have been the architect of one of the most diabolical sports rivalry strategies in the north. Whitehorse and Skagway had a friendly rivalry in baseball, basketball, and hockey and sent teams back and forth on the railroad on a regular basis for the previous 40 years. Someone (Mary?) convinced the train engineers that they needed to extend their time in Carcross on each journey preceding the games.

The short delay in departing enabled the traveling team to run over to the Caribou and buy a few cases of beer for the ride either to Whitehorse or Skagway. It was common for the first game to be played shortly after the train's arrival at its destination and the Carcross beer stop ensured the visiting team was in no sober shape to win the series opener.

The teams from Skagway and Whitehorse probably both recognized the tactical aspect of the extended stop but both sides fell happily into the trap every time.

There was no extended stop for the team trains on the return journey.

She and June also figured out how to run the bar without a barmaid or bartender when they were shorthanded – which was almost all the time. They set a 45-gallon drum filled with ice and beer in the middle of the floor. The customer would pick a bottle out of the ice and pay for it by putting cash in a small box on the bar. It was an honour system the regular patrons were expected to self-police – and they did so religiously because if they didn't there was hell to pay.

If the money in the box and the number of beer missing from the barrel didn't add up, the barrel was removed for the next week and the drinkers were subjected to the wrath of the bartender – who could compete with Polly in all the colourful aspects of the English language.

June did the cooking – was particularly good at preparing fish dishes, especially lake trout which she bought from the local commercial fishermen – and looked after room rentals and housekeeping. She never brought up the subject of a kitchen apparition.

A childhood pal of Mary's from her Nanaimo days, Dorothy Hopcott, came north in 1955 with her husband George. She leased the beer parlour in the Regina Hotel in Whitehorse but gave that up after George ran off with one of the barmaids. It didn't take long for Mary to talk her despondent friend into moving to Carcross and helping with the hotel.

Dorothy bought out June's share of the business in 1959 when June moved to Bennett to cook for the WPYR. When June married another White Pass employee, John Klein, a couple of years later they booked the hotel for the wedding reception.

In 1964, Dorothy purchased Mary's share of the Caribou when Mary decided it was time to do something different somewhere else.

It was probably the following year when Dorothy started to notice that the kitchen might have another, less material occupant.

Dorothy never saw any apparition in the kitchen nor apparently has anyone else. It was the red handle on the stove that alerted her to his presence.

The handle turned the gas off during the night so there would be no propane leaking into the hotel while she slept. The last thing she did every night after cleaning up the kitchen, putting everything away, and organizing what she might need in the morning, was turn it to the "off" position.

One morning she noticed the handle returned to the "on" position. Once or twice might have been a night-before oversight on her part, but almost every morning started to make her nervous. Some days she found the stove lit and the flame set at the right level to perk a pot of coffee.

Initially, like most people, she was skeptical about the idea of a haunting but years of no other plausible explanation and other occurrences – not in the kitchen – finally convinced her to accept the possibility.

It had to be a mess sergeant, Dorothy and her husband Don McLellan finally decided, because anyone who used the kitchen before the war wouldn't have the knowledge of how to turn on the stove, which was installed in 1942. After Dorothy and Don sold the hotel in 1980 there was no further evidence of the mess sergeant's presence.

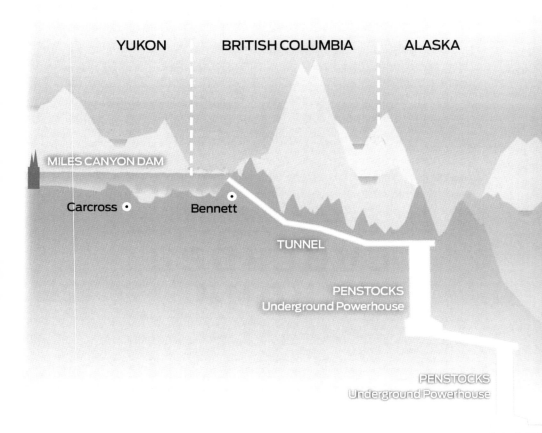

YUKON   BRITISH COLUMBIA   ALASKA

MILES CANYON DAM

Carcross •   Bennett •

TUNNEL

PENSTOCKS
Underground Powerhouse

PENSTOCKS
Underground Powerhouse

Dyea

The Taiya Project

Chapter 22

THE
PLOT
TO
DROWN
CARCROSS

Some of the people who stayed in the Caribou during the late 1940s and early '50s had a rather more nefarious reason for doing so than simply visiting Carcross. They were trying to figure out how to submerge the town under 18 metres (60 feet) of water.

Two people came up with the idea about the same time.

Apparently, the first was a Canadian mining promoter and developer named Thayer Lindsley. His idea was to construct a series of dams that could create an 800-kilometre (500-mile） lake reaching from the coastal mountains to Fort Selkirk, capturing the flow of both the Yukon and Pelly Rivers and all of the southern lakes.

The largest and most important dam would be built at Miles Canyon near Whitehorse. The dams would reverse the flow of the Yukon River and redirect the water through a series of tunnels drilled under the coastal mountains to a hydro station on Taku Inlet, close to Juneau, Alaska. The project had the potential to meet the growing need for energy in both the territory of Alaska and the United States in addition to providing power at reduced rates for any mine that Thayer was investing in.

The proposed lake would permanently flood Carcross, Atlin, Bennett, and Tagish.

It's unlikely that any of Thayer's people stayed at the Caribou while researching the proposal. His was a fanciful flight of fantasy that once voiced was almost as quickly forgotten. He was a successful mining visionary, not a builder of dams.

The second one to come up with the idea was R.C. Johnson, an engineer working for the US government's Bureau of Reclamation in 1946.

Following the end of the Second World War and the dawning of the "Cold War" the US military determined that maintaining a strategic presence in Alaska was vital to national security. The Soviet Union (USSR) was just across the Bering Strait from Alaska and many saw the territory as a natural route for invasion or simply a space over which missiles could fly to their intended targets in the United States should the Cold War turn hot.

There was a shortage of hydro sites in Alaska and more electricity was required than was available. The Department of the Interior asked the Bureau of Reclamation if they would identify resources that might be of value in developing Alaska's economy and mounting a potential defence in the event of aggression by the USSR.

Johnson studied the idea of harnessing the hydro potential of the Yukon River and came up with the Tagish-Lynn Project, later renamed The Taiya Project.

It differed from Thayer Lindsley's project in two ways. First, there would be only one massive dam – at Miles Canyon. The proposed lake would be shorter but deeper. The tunnels would go under the Chilkoot Trail and come out in Taiya Inlet near the former town of Dyea.

Coincidently, the name Taiya comes from a Tlingit word, Tayee, which means "underneath".

The other major difference was that it wasn't a flight of fancy quickly forgotten. The US government did initially shelve the idea but only until it was discovered by corporate America.

The project caught the eye of the Aluminum Company of America (ALCOA) in 1947. ALCOA was the world's largest producer of aluminum but had started branching out into the production of energy following the war. They modified Johnson's plan somewhat, adding a proposed aluminum plant in the Taiya Valley, along with a small town to house the employees and a small hydro station at Miles Canyon to provide power for Whitehorse.

Because of the interest expressed by ALCOA the Bureau of Reclamation sent two engineers to the Yukon and Alaska to study the viability of the proposal in greater detail.

They were the first to take a room at the Caribou with the express intention of filling it with water.

The power potential of the Taiya Project, they concluded, was substantially greater than a dam of comparable size built on another North American river could produce. Their report resulted in the US Geological Survey classifying Taiya Inlet as a power site in 1948.

Negotiations were complex because the project affected water crossing an international border — not just where the project was planned to be built but also further north where damming the Yukon River would affect its natural flow into Alaska.

The Canadian government was intrigued by the enthusiasm and determination of ALCOA in pursuing the project despite bureaucratic hurdles on both side of the border and, in 1949, withdrew from potential disposal of any lands in the Whitehorse area and southern lakes region that might be covered by the lake — which was everything below 2,215 feet (675 metres) above sea level.

Local resistance was already brewing. The people of Carcross and Atlin weren't happy about possibly losing their homes. The WPYR protested because it meant a large chunk of their railroad and the pipeline paralleling it ended up underwater potentially putting them out of business. The residents of Whitehorse got upset when the US Bureau of Mines suggested evacuating and inundating that town as well.

Carcross only had three buildings in its downtown — the Caribou, Mathew Watson's Store, and the train station — but there was also an airfield and a US Army fuel tank farm as well as the approximately 50 private log homes on both sides of the narrows. All of which would have to be relocated or drowned.

Bennett had multiple installations in place that would have to be moved uphill. Almost 50 kilometres (30 miles) of railroad would have to be relocated above the proposed high water mark. Nine miles of the Alaska Highway would be under the lake as would the entire Alcan Highway built by the 93rd Engineers between Carcross and Jake's Corner.

By this time ALCOA had topographical and hydrological survey crews working out of Skagway, Carcross, and Whitehorse. Planes flew off the Carcross airfield to take aerial photos along the length of the lakes and rivers. Handwritten notes on the photos suggest building the main dam at Miles Canyon as originally envisioned. Maps were produced setting out plans to relocate the train tracks and pipeline above the high-water mark and ensure continued access to Skagway from Whitehorse.

A joint economic committee, consisting of representatives from the Canadian, US, and British Columbia governments, visited the communities to determine the impact the project might have on the region.

With all the activity the Caribou, with its bar, café and rooms, was reaping a nice profit from those who were planning her demise.

In 1951, the Canadian government, decided against the Taiya Project. This decision was based on a report by geologist Hugh Bostock in which he argued against the use of Canadian water to generate power for American corporations with little or no compensation for Canada.

However, ALCOA and Alaska were persistent. ALCOA reiterated in 1952 that they were going to proceed with the project, renaming it the Yukon River Power Diversion Project, and started lobbying the US State Department to convince them that the US simply had to offer something in trade to Canada in exchange for the water rights affecting Taiya. What they were going to trade and how the US was supposed to do that, ALCOA left up to the politicians.

Alaskan politicians sought the approval of US President Harry Truman. Since the CANOL project had helped put him in the White House in 1945 someone probably figured he might be convinced that building Taiya would be a crowning achievement for his administration and a major step in winning statehood for Alaska.

Truman was interested but insisted the project not be turned over to private corporations. Every power project, he said, needed to "be done to keep them in the public interest." He approved a report to go to Congress for debate but finished his presidency without acting on the Taiya Project.

The Alaskans tried a media blitz to persuade the public that Taiya was a project worthy of support with newspapers from New York to Nome running lengthy articles about the magnitude and benefits of the project.

In 1954, Frobisher Ltd., a Canadian mining company, applied for a water rights license for the portion of the Yukon River in British Columbia to try and kick-start the process again in Canada.

It wasn't enough. The Canadian government refused to budge and, in 1957, ALCOA announced the Taiya Project was dead.

After 1954 Yukon politicians referred to Taiya as the Frobisher Plan because of Frobisher Ltd.'s involvement.

There were plenty of boats available in case lake levels were raised

According to the minutes of a meeting of Yukon politicians and bureaucrats in Whitehorse in January, 1970, the lands potentially covered by the lake and withdrawn by the federal government from disposal in 1949 were still being withheld.

Following the discussion about developing housing lots in Carcross, assistant commissioner C.W. Fleming wrote, "How many firms have indicated they will build homes in Carcross – only Venus – the local hotel will be arranging accommodation and feeding for the single man – restrictions re number of businesses – a carry-over from the Frobisher plan... check on the Federal policy re leasing of land below a certain benchmark...according to Gordon McIntyre the Order in Council is still in effect... land below 2,215 is still being withheld."

Despite the restrictions, Fleming's notes go on to say, the territorial government was preparing to receive requests for the land and the Frobisher plan was of "secondary importance."

Chapter 23

WHAT IS A COMMUNITY WITHOUT A HOTEL?

"The hotel is vital to the small town," said Archie Lang in 2017, after three decades of owning hotels in small northern communities. "It is the hub of the community. Whether it's Carcross, Ross River or Keno City. If you don't have a hotel you don't have a community. If you don't have one, where do people go to have a cup of coffee? To talk and socialize on neutral ground?"

A conference held in 2016 for individuals and corporations who owned hotels in small rural communities in the United States focused on the concept that hotels in small-town America give small-town America its identity. The same notion applied to Canada, in particular, to the more isolated communities in the north where the role of the community hotel was, more often than not, much larger than just being a hotel.

Part of the Scott Hotel, before it burned down in 1936, had been turned into a classroom when the number of students outgrew the Carcross school. There were no rooms large enough to hold community meetings in Carcross in the 1960s except for the bar in the Caribou Hotel. Even the circuit court – the Yukon Government's travelling community court trial system – used it.

Beer line-up at the Carcross Inn, 1942

"It was like the wild west," recalled Larry McLellan in 2018. He had been called as a witness in a case involving a car accident on Montana Mountain. "The judge sat at one table in his mackinaw shirt, work pants and boots. The lawyers at poker tables on either side of him. Nobody wore suits or ties. There was a chair for the witness to testify from. Everyone else just stood or sat around the back of the room. I think some of them weren't there for the proceedings but were waiting for everything to get finished so the bar would reopen."

In order to succeed, the conference attendees agreed, the hotel couldn't stand alone as an independent entity. It had to be run in collaboration with the community with everyone working toward a common goal. The primary motivation for owning the business cannot be for making money. It must be, above all else, an investment made to help the community.

Without that mindset and the links it formed with the community, the venture would be doomed to failure. History showed that approach to be essential in rural sustainability for both the hotel and the community.

Community businesses needed to retain revenue that otherwise might have been lost to local people buying commodities or services from nearby, larger towns. Being profitable helped local government retain tax revenues, enabling them to maintain required infrastructure like water and sewage, garbage collection, and roads as well as providing services like garbage collection.

There was a necessity to generate new revenue by providing services for visiting professionals, employees, customers, and visitors who might otherwise just keep heading on down the road to a warm bed elsewhere.

Horses, cattle and chickens freely wandered the streets of Carcross in the 1970s, often hanging around the Caribou Hotel

Local families also desired accommodations and space when friends and family are coming to town for a wedding, funeral, reunion or just to visit. No space in town could mean the event might have to be held elsewhere or in a community space less suitable to the circumstance.

The Caribou Hotel was Carcross's social and commercial center

It wasn't uncommon for weddings and funerals to be held in the Caribou. There were two churches in Carcross but they were small buildings and couldn't hold many people.

Clubs, organizations, sport tournaments and non-profits require meeting spaces and rooms for special events or unique attractions.

In the 1980s, the Yukon Sports Federation used the Caribou restaurant as a checkpoint during the Trail of '98 International Road Relay (a footrace from Skagway to Whitehorse that attracts runners from around the world) in September of each year.

"It was a great place to hang out while waiting for your team to arrive," said one competitor in 1985. "The exchange for the runners was right outside the front door. They kept the restaurant open all night for the volunteers and put on extra coffee and breakfasts for the runners while we waited for our teams to arrive. You could socialize with the people

'Klondike Kate' Rockwell disembarked from the train in Carcross in the 1940s and went to the Caribou for a drink

you knew or meet someone new – whatever you wanted to do. There were probably a lot of relationships, marriages, and friendships that started in that place."

There was in small communities an integral need for a place where locals could simply gather to sip coffee, quaff a beer, watch a hockey game on TV or enjoy a meal they didn't have to cook.

The future, the hoteliers' conference keynote speaker stated, was no longer in providing material souvenirs to visitors but in giving them unforgettable experiences. People would rather have a quality sense-of-place experience, he said, than spend their money buying another item. An interesting hotel in an intriguing place with unique events or attractions – like a haunting – could become a major destination.

Mrs. Gideon would probably have agreed with that conclusion.

Chapter 24

DOROTHY
AND
DON

Many people, tourists and locals alike, often commented that going into the Caribou was like going into Dorothy Hopcott's home – because in truth that was exactly what they were doing.

Dorothy lived in the owner's suite directly over the front door. The suite was two rooms that had been modified to be a large, single room with a bed, a sitting area, and an office. It was not only the largest room on the upper floors of the hotel it was also the warmest in winter.

The chimney from the large wood-burning furnace, located in the crawl space under the hotel, ran up through one corner of the room and radiated plenty of warmth for the suite. All the other rooms depended upon heat that might seep into them from the hallway. There was a sort-of forced-air heating system, which helped a bit. It was a large circulating fan that pulled the heat, along with the smell of stale beer and thick blue clouds of cigarette smoke from the bar, and pushed it through a vent into the upstairs hallways.

"It was cold in those rooms," recalled Arthur Mitchell who traveled to Carcross in the winter and spring for curling bonspiels in the 1970s. "It was like winter camping outdoors in the snow with a light sleeping bag. You got more heat from shivering then you ever did from the hallway."

It wasn't uncommon in winter for all the water pipes on the windward side of the hotel to freeze when the winds blew off Bennett Lake against the lightly insulated walls. The hotel acted like a sail and rocked back and forth as the wind built and ebbed, with cold air finding its way indoors through every nook, cranny, and crack.

"The hotel was nothing more than a windbreak for anyone who wanted to get out of those winds," said Archie Lang, who leased the hotel over the winter of 1969-70. "It was cold as the hubs of hell – that place. I burned hundreds of cords of wood that winter. All day and all night I had to go down into the crawl space every few hours and throw more logs into the furnace."

The café and kitchen were heated by the old army cook stove and the bar had its own small wood-burning barrel stove beside the bar.

The café was not only where Dorothy cooked for and served customers, it was her personal eating area and where she ironed the room linens. A person dropping by for coffee and pie might be expected to lend a hand folding the sheets after she swiped the final wrinkle out of them.

She never ran out of willing customers to help her because the Caribou became famous for its pie and ice cream and there was a steady stream of people all day long – train passengers flocking around Polly, tired and dusty people who had just finished the drive from Whitehorse, and the locals who had nowhere else to go after the Carcross Inn closed in 1960.

On extremely busy days, if all they wanted was coffee and pie, she told people just to help themselves and leave the money on the table. It would also be helpful if when they were done they could put their dirty dishes in the sink in the kitchen, thank you.

If a person came in who couldn't afford to pay for his or her meal or simply didn't have the money in their pocket at that time, she served them anyway, waving off their shortage of funds by saying, "Next time." Most turned up later to pay their delinquent bill but for some of them who couldn't afford to buy a meal, "next time" never came. Dorothy kept serving them anyway, saying "next time" every time.

"She cared for the people in the community. She loved Carcross and the people," said Anne Morgan, "And they loved her."

The dining area had windows on two walls, creating a good atmosphere for a summer greenhouse, so Dorothy established a full wall of plants along one side. Polly lived in the front room where she had the steam ironing board set up. When she got into a nasty mood, as Polly could, she swore at Dorothy who then dissolved into tears and covered the cage.

When television finally arrived in Carcross in the late 1960s, Dorothy set one up in the bar and immediately got hooked on afternoon soap operas – initially it was Days of Our Lives and in the 1970s, The Young and Restless. A customer coming into the hotel between two or three in the afternoon could watch the "soaps" with her but didn't expect any service until the show was over.

If the customer wanted to talk to someone while Dorothy was watching TV they sat down with Johnnie Johns.

Johnnie had mostly retired from the outfitting business in 1969 but still did the odd guiding trip for the new owners of his business and for his old friends who found their way north. When he wasn't outfitting or travelling somewhere in the world to visit friends or former clients he could be found at the Caribou telling stories and reciting poetry.

However, he discovered that, with his advancing years, the chairs in the café and the bar weren't as comfortable as they were in his younger days. He carried his own personal chair to the hotel in the morning and packed it back home each night. On sunny summer days he would position his seat on the wooden slat sidewalk in front of the hotel, alongside Polly who was placed outside in the sun by Dorothy or Don. In the winters and on rainy summer days it and he went into the bar or café.

Students at the Carcross Community Education Centre had reason to appreciate the McLellan's community spirit. The Centre was located in the former Chout'la Residential School, which closed in 1969. The "hippie school", as the locals called the Centre, was to help high school students from just about anywhere who struggled with the traditional structure of the education system. It introduced them to a broader sense of education in a communal setting.

Its most notable feature, according to former students, was that it had a laundry facility that was more renowned for shredding clothes than cleaning them. The Centre closed for good in 1979.

Former student Daphne Mennell remembered Dorothy and her husband Don cooking Christmas dinner for the students because "most of us were from somewhere else and either couldn't or didn't go home for Christmas." One of the hotel regulars, Shorty Schroder, waited tables for the students.

Don McLellan turned up in Dorothy's life in 1966.

In the early 1930s, while studying engineering at university, he earned tuition money as an enforcer for a bootlegging gang based in his home province of New Brunswick. Don wasn't a big man but he was as tough as they come. People who shirked their debts to the bootleggers paid up quickly rather than tangling with him. When he finished his education there wasn't much call for engineers so he headed west. Don hopped freight trains to get from town to town and learned how to cook in the hobo camps. People found or were given food and they brought it to him to be cooked in exchange for sharing their meal with him.

When war came he enlisted in the Royal Canadian Engineers and was with them when they landed on Juno Beach during the June 6, 1944, D-Day invasion of Europe. His experience as an enforcer came in handy as he took up the sport of boxing. He was good enough to get into the ring in a bout for the Canadian Army boxing championship, but not good enough to win.

A gold company hired him to work at the Braelorn Mine in southern British Columbia in the early 1960s where he gained a reputation as an "honest" miner — which meant an employer could trust him to do the work without "high grading" or smuggling stolen gold out of the mines.

Braelorn was also where he learned he needed to get his drinking under control. In a bar fight one night he almost killed his opponent. It terrified him that he didn't remember why they got into the fight in the first place nor when he lost control of himself during the fight. He didn't completely quit drinking but after that night he never drank to excess again.

Eventually his engineering background came in handy as he became part owner of Canadian Mine Services and won the contract to construct a road from Carcross to the Venus Mine on Montana Mountain, close to the ruins of Conrad.

"I came to Carcross in 1966," Don told author Ursula Heller for her book Village Portraits, "on June 7, at seven o'clock at night. I went into the bar, drank some whiskey and fell in love with Dorothy."

Once he met Dorothy it didn't take long for him to quit his job and get involved with both her and the hotel.

In the morning he cooked breakfast for the guests. For part of the day he was the maintenance man, making sure that everything that Dorothy needed to run the hotel, like unplugged toilets, operated the way it was supposed to. There was always something to do.

One day he discovered there was a problem with the bathtub on the second floor. One of the guests decided to use the old tub in the communal bathroom, put the plug in, filled it with hot water, and had himself a nice soak.

When he was finished he pulled the plug and the tub emptied its contents into the bar below. It turned out that at some point the drain pipe for the tub had been removed but it was rarely used so its absence had gone unnoticed until now.

On most days he set nets in Bennett and Tagish Lakes to catch fish so Dorothy would have something to serve her customers for dinner.

When the day's work was done he took up his favourite position in a comfortable rocking chair near the woodstove after opening the bar in the early afternoon.

When the Army used the hotel as a mess hall, they opened up the bar and reception areas into one large dining area, leaving only a small room at the end which housed the bar. Dorothy added a wall to divide the mess hall in half, making one segment a café and the other portion, the hotel lobby and bar. The small area that used to be the Army bar she left intact to comply with the law of the time which demanded that men and women enter using the appropriate entryway and drink in different parts of the lounge.

Dorothy Hopcott with carving of Polly by artist Gary Sam

From his vantage point by the stove, Don could see all the entrances into the bar, be aware of what might be happening on the other side of the wall where the ladies were, and keep an eye on the behaviour of the bar patrons. If someone got intoxicated and became unruly, they were banned from the hotel.

Don tended bar on his own terms. When a customer ordered a cocktail or a beer Don kept rocking, exchanging gossip, and passing the time of day until he figured it was time to get up, go behind the bar, and pour the drink. If the person was banned from the hotel or Don figured he or she was too inebriated already he just kept rocking and talking without ever getting up to pour a drink.

His reputation as a fighter preceded him. None ever challenged his authority in the bar.

He was probably a match for storytelling with Johnnie Johns. They frequently swapped tales although Don didn't do the animated acting and few, if any, of his canards were true.

Years later, when Dorothy was asked to recall her time as owner of the Caribou, Don kept interrupting her dialogue with almost believable stories of his own. Each time Dorothy listened patiently then gave him a light swat, saying, "Oh Don, shut-up. You know that's not true. You should stop making stuff up." Then continued on with her reminiscences with Don lurking in the background, waiting to pounce with another tall tale.

Despite Don's attempts to inflate the truth or distort it entirely, Dorothy recalled hosting gatherings in the hotel chaired by the Prime Minister of Canada, Pierre Elliot Trudeau, on two occasions – 1969 and 1977. A future Prime Minister, Jean Chrétien, also spent a night in the hotel in 1975 when he was the federal minister of Northern Affairs.

Because it was the midway point on the railroad the executive of the White Pass and Yukon Route used the Caribou as a base whenever they were overseeing any crisis or simply wanted to hold a meeting in interesting surroundings.

To accommodate the volume of guests she was getting Dorothy set up two trailer units on the lot previously occupied by the Carcross Inn, in which she was able to construct an additional eight rooms with a shared washroom and shower.

All the wastewater was piped into a septic field behind the hotel. When the field was covered in the autumn with hay to insulate it from the winter cold, the abundance of available feed attracted two cows who wandered down the road and ate all the insulation.

View from the Caribou Hotel bar in the 1970s

The Caribou itself was starting to show its age. Dorothy didn't think that, other than the modifications the US Army did in 1942, any renovation or structural repairs had ever been done to the hotel since it was built. Rather than taking on the task herself she came up with innovative solutions.

In the summer of 1973 Whitehorse-based engineer Tim Keopke was working near Carcross and staying at the Caribou. On his first night, just as he headed up the stairs to his room, Dorothy handed him a bundle of brown paper towels.

"What are these for?" asked Tim, "Are there no towels in the room?"

"They're to stop the smoke from getting into your room," she explained. "Just wet them and lay them down over the cracks on the floorboards."

People still smoked cigarettes in bars in 1973 and the air in the small lounge was literally blue. The smoke found its way up through the stamped metal ceiling tiles and into the rooms above through gaps between the old floorboards.

"It worked," recalled Tim more than four decades later. "I would get down on the floor every night and cover all the cracks with the wet paper towels and they stopped the smoke from getting into my room."

He also remembered waking up under a threadbare patchwork quilt on his first morning in the hotel, climbing out of the painted brass frame bed that sagged in the centre, and wondering why the floor felt so damp and clammy. He had forgotten all about the paper towels.

Mrs. Gideon was as much a reality for Don and Dorothy as the Army mess sergeant in the kitchen. Fortunately, one night, when they were awakened by a presence by their bedside, they were already familiar with many stories from local residents about seeing her in a third-floor window overlooking the train station.

At some point in the late 1960s Dorothy apparently met the dead trapper on the third floor. She asked Don to board up the staircase to the third floor and never open it again, without ever satisfactorily explaining her reasons for the closure.

She may have thought the third floor spirit was Mary Tobacco's friend Jens Olsen. He also had been a trapper, physically broken by his livelihood and advanced in age. When Mary didn't think he was capable of looking after himself she brought him into the hotel where he spent his final days in a third-storey room.

Whomever it was, it appears that for Dorothy it was one ghost too many.

Faro Ore Truck was symbolic of the booming mining industry in the Yukon in the late 1970s

Chapter 25

BOOM
TO
BUST

When Archie Lang took over the management of the Caribou in 1969 it was "a mad house."

"Carcross was a busy place. The town jumped," said Lang. "We had the railroad. Ninety per cent of the people in Carcross worked for White Pass. They would go out to their work cams at Bennett, Pennington, and Fraser for the week, then come in on the weekend and spend a lot of time in the bar and restaurant.

"There was mining exploration for the Arctic (Gold and Silver Corporation) and Venus Mines (a venture to open new mines on Montana Mountain above the abandoned Conrad City location). The pipeline between Whitehorse and Skagway was still being used to bring fuel into the Yukon. In the summer they had crews cutting and creosoting ties for the railroad.

"The Caribou was a working man's hotel. It was a White Pass hotel. It was a mining hotel because during the summer we would always have some geologists staying there, some miners and exploration crews.

"The Yukon government was looking to enhance the road between Carcross and the Venus Mine and the federal government was surveying the boundary between Canada and the United States so we had survey crews and archaeologists staying in the hotel.

"There would be two passenger trains through during the day then three or four more at night. They were hauling ore for the mines."

The Yukon was experiencing a mining upsurge unlike anything ever seen before in the north and Carcross was reaping all the benefits of a small town at the centre of an economic boom.

The industry had long been aware that shipping ore to Whitehorse, loading it on the railroad to take it to tidewater at Skagway, then by ship down to refineries in Trail, BC, was not just the most efficient way to get their product out of the territory – it was the only way.

All of the gold mined in the Klondike since 1896 had left the Yukon on the WPYR. All the gold from Engineer Mine and silver/lead/zinc from the Big Thing Mine, along with copper from the Copper King and Pueblo Mines near Whitehorse, was shipped out by rail between 1903 and 1916.

United Keno Hill Mines, for four decades North America's largest silver producer and fourth largest in the world, had been transporting ore on the railroad since 1947. Mineral explorations and discoveries in the 1950s and early 1960s resulted in several mines opening in the Yukon, starting with Cassiar Asbestos establishing a mine at Clinton Creek, 100 kilometres north of Dawson City.

New Imperial Mines started mining copper in the Whitehorse Copper Belt in 1967 and three years later the railroad's single biggest customer, the Cyprus Anvil Mining Corporation, came on-line. Their lead/zinc mine in Faro, Yukon, was the largest in Canada and one of the largest in the world. When the price of gold was deregulated in 1973, numerous existing gold mines that had been on the verge of mothballing their operations were suddenly viable and valuable once again.

The idea of a road link through the mountains between Carcross and Skagway had been floating around since the completion of the railroad in 1900. People who couldn't afford to buy a ticket from Skagway or Whitehorse would walk the tracks and occasionally, one would get run over by the train.

The Duchess train engine at work between Atlin and Tagish Lakes

The tracks had witnessed a particularly large amount of pedestrian traffic during the 1930s as desperate people flocked north looking for work in the gold fields of the Klondike, which had escaped the decade largely unscathed by the Great Depression.

The 1905 survey of the road from Carcross to Conrad and Wynton actually went beyond those locations to Log Cabin, a maintenance camp on the railway close to the US-Canada border. More survey work and slashing was done in 1913, and again in 1920, despite opposition from the WPYR, who saw a road as competition in the freight-hauling business.

Nothing concrete was done until 1961 when a group of volunteers, along with the Alaskan government, started blasting a road into the granite walls of the coastal mountains across the valley from the railway tracks. That effort eventually petered out when the BC government refused to fund the 58 kilometres of road that would run through that province.

The construction of a bridge for cars and trucks across the Nares River in 1970 sparked a revival of the idea. Prior to the new crossing, the only way for vehicles to navigate the narrows was to use the railroad bridge. The drawbridge that used to cross the narrows as part of the wagon road to Conrad had long ago been dismantled.

The Yukon's last wooden bridge was built across the narrows at Carcross to move ore from Yukon mines to tide water

The WPYR constantly attempted to ban vehicular traffic on the train bridge for safety and insurance concerns. The last thing they wanted was somebody trying to beat the train across the bridge and not making it.

In 1974, the Alaskan, BC, and Yukon governments decided to complete the road and two years later work began in earnest. Despite legal challenges from the WPYR and a 1977 conflict with the Carcross Indian Band over access through their land, it was unofficially opened in 1978 as a summer road only, intended only for light tourist traffic. The official dedication happened in May, 1981, near Skagway at a spot called Liar's Camp.

The road construction crews filled the rooms and café at the Caribou for almost two years.

There seemed to be no end in sight for the good times until, without warning, world mineral prices collapsed in 1981, rendering every major mine in the Yukon virtually worthless almost overnight.

Cassiar Asbestos had already closed the Clinton Creek Mine in 1978.

United Keno Hill Mines, which had just invested a lot of money into a potential mine and processing mill near the Venus Mine site, called a halt to the project in 1981 and laid off most of their employees from their mines. The company limped along for a few more years but was finally forced into bankruptcy in 1990.

Whitehorse Copper stopped mining new ore when the price of copper plummeted and only processed what they had already dug out of the ground. They closed their doors for good on Dec. 31, 1982, after depleting their stockpile.

Cyprus Anvil shut down the Faro mine completely in 1981.

Only the gold mines persisted because gold values were still reasonably high but they represented merely a minute fraction of the ore being shipped out of the Yukon.

A system of trucking ore from the mines to Whitehorse then simply lifting the ore container from the truck and placing it on a flatbed rail car had been very efficient for both the mines and the railroad.

Planned upgrades to the road to Skagway threated to provide possible competition for what small bits of hauling business that still existed. When the WPYR shut down the railroad almost all of the workers in Carcross found themselves out of a job.

The road to Whitehorse was upgraded and paved in 1982-83 making it more convenient and less expensive to make the trip to Whitehorse for groceries and alcohol. Business at both Mathew Watson's Store and the Caribou dried up.

With employment becoming scarce thousands of Yukoners packed up and headed south as the territory headed into the longest, deepest depression in its history.

Not until Mount Skookum, a gold and silver mine close to Carcross in the mountains above the Wheaton River Valley, opened in 1986 was there a glimmer of hope. However, even that venture was essentially mothballed after only two years and provided little in terms of real benefit to the town.

Curragh Resources acquired the Faro mine previously operated by Cyprus Anvil in 1986 but made reopening it conditional on upgrading and maintaining the road to Skagway to accommodate heavy truck traffic year-round. The mining company also paid a maintenance fee to subsidize the expense of keeping the road open.

The Yukon government, desperate for any kind of economic stimulus, agreed. The WPYR went into the trucking business hauling ore to tidewater and carrying fuel and freight on the backhaul to the Yukon.

Curraugh shipped ore south from Faro until 1993 when the company was forced into bankruptcy in the wake of a tragedy that claimed 26 lives in an explosion at its Westray Coal Mine in Nova Scotia.

The WPYR based its trucking operations in Whitehorse and Skagway, bypassing Carcross entirely.

When the railroad was started up again in 1988 for summers only it ran daily trips for cruise ship passengers from Skagway to the summit of the White Pass and return. In 1990, the run was extended to Bennett where passengers stopped for lunch then re-boarded for the return trip to Skagway.

Not until July, 1997, when a special charter to celebrate the 100th anniversary of the Klondike Gold Rush pulled into the station, was the melancholy blowing of the steam whistle heard once gain echoing in the mountains surrounding Carcross.

It was a romantic summons that hadn't changed in over 100 years and its haunting melody sent shivers down the backs of all who heard it.

Chapter 26

RAY OLSON'S VISION

Ray Olson bought the Caribou Hotel by mistake.

He was a fairly successful building contractor in Vancouver in the 1970s. When Dorothy Thorsen approached him in 1980 to go into partnership with her and co-sign a bank loan so she could buy a hotel in some place he had never heard of, he agreed.

Ray had no intention of moving north and becoming a hotel operator. Other than some time spent cooking on a coastal ferry when he was younger, he knew nothing about the hospitality industry. Dorothy would run the Caribou while he continued with his contracting business in Vancouver and, at first, that's how it went.

Then Dorothy quit the partnership for reasons unknown sometime in late 1981 or early 1982. Her sudden departure left Ray with a hotel and an outstanding bank loan.

Contracting was hard work and Ray wasn't a young man anymore. The hotel had produced good revenues over the previous two years so he decided to shut down his business in Vancouver and move north. His son Bob, a part-time truck driver, also moved to Carcross.

Ray Olson on the stairs to the third floor

Ray had the makings of a good small-town hotelier – a great sense of humour, good people skills, and he knew his way around the kitchen – but his timing was lousy.

Interest rates on bank loans were around 24% in the early 1980s and the fallout from the 1981 mining crash – no jobs, no railroad, and almost no tourism – hamstrung the business. Ray drained his life's savings then fell behind on his loan payments and property tax.

He leased the hotel to Bev and Lionel Hart for six months. The Harts proved to be good managers, submitting their lease payments on time despite the hard times. Bev also threw Bob out of the bar on a regular basis because he was drunk all the time. Eventually, Bob moved back to Vancouver.

When the lease expired Ray took over the business again but by 1987 he was on the verge of bankruptcy.

When Vern Smuk, Ethel Tizya, and Hilda Popadynec approached Ray with an offer to lease the hotel he jumped at the opportunity. Vern and Hilda entered into a lease-to-purchase in April, 1987.

Ray thought he had solved his insolvency problem but Vern had other ideas.

In October, 1987, he and Hilda filed a lawsuit in which they claimed ownership of the Caribou by virtue of their lease-to-purchase option. According to Dorothy Hopcott, Vern and Hilda were willing to pay $30,000 to cover overdue taxes and loan payments rather than the $200,000 agreed upon purchase price in exchange for title to the property.

The territorial court denied their claim instead appointing Dale Schmekel to act as an administrator/manager. Dale was a friend of Ray's and had assisted him with meeting his immediate cash-flow needs.

Chairs, a bed frame and mattresses (far right) in storage. The third floor was used to store furniture no longer needed or wanted

The two men became friends when former Saskatchewan premier Allan Blakeney came to the Yukon to speak at the New Democratic Party (NDP) convention in Whitehorse in 1983. Dale convinced Blakeney to take a trip down the dusty gravel road to Carcross, which was also under construction in preparation for being paved, just to have lunch in the Caribou. Ray, a life-long NDPer, had been tickled pink and cooked up his specialty, fresh lake trout, for his guests.

Dale operated the hotel until early 1992 when a bar customer "mooned" his wife and she decided enough was enough. He closed the hotel for the summer of 1992 but it reopened in September that year when Alice and Dean McGuire signed a lease.

Ray worked as a contractor wherever and whenever he could and Dale helped him make payments to the bank and eventually catch up on the taxes in arrears. In 1994, Dale successfully asked the territorial court to remove himself as the administrator and restore Ray as the owner of the Caribou.

The Olsons sued Vern Smuk for damages and won a $60,000 judgement against him, which was, according to Bob, "the largest award for punitive damages in Canadian history." They never collected a cent of it.

Yet, Dorothy Hopcott recalled, Vern wasn't completely out of the picture yet. Even though he was not the owner of the Caribou he was allegedly trying to sell shares in the business – shares that didn't exist and which he wouldn't have owned even if they had. It apparently took a visit from the law to stop him and eventually he left the Yukon.

Ray had big plans for the Caribou. In 1981, he outlined his intention to give the Yukon's second-oldest hotel a facelift and restore it to its former glory. The renovation and expansion of the hotel would create local construction jobs and the modern hotel would need a lot of staff to operate.

There was a lot of work to do to bring it up to snuff. The plumbing had to be totally removed and replaced. Some walls were coming out because they were rotting away. The flowered linoleum in the dining area was almost worn through and the bathroom fixtures and walls were old and stained. The middle of the hotel was sagging because, as Ray discovered, the hotel had been constructed without a centre weight-bearing beam. It was surprising it hadn't collapsed under its own weight already.

The dip in the floor gave the hotel the appearance that it was slowly sinking. Windowsills that had been constructed at a person's waist height were now almost at ground level and there was a step down from the sidewalk in front to enter the front doors. The doors had once been at the same level as the sidewalk.

The furniture in the rooms on the second floor was old. Solid oak dressers badly in need of refurbishing. Brass lamps with shades that hung in tatters. Window curtains dangled like old, wet, worn-out dishrags. Tarnished mirrors. Brass rail beds, covered with black paint, sagging in the middle.

Ray opened up the third floor for the first time since Dorothy Hopcott demanded it be closed off more than 20 years earlier. Dorothy and Don may not have allowed guests to stay there but they hadn't let the space go to waste. It was a maze of collected antiques. The rooms and halls jam-packed with bureaus, mirrors, wolverine and marten pelts, moose antlers, framed photographs, an old gramophone with boxes of thick, black 78 rpm records, and piles of magazines.

In the bar were large round oak tables and an antique poker table scarred by 80 years of beer bottles and cigarette burns. An old jukebox in one corner still worked well except that there was no way to turn down the volume. Ancient stuffed moose heads, with their hair falling out and decorated for some long-forgotten purpose with feathers, gazed down at the pool table.

Saved from the flames by the Gideons in 1909 and played by the black soldiers in 1942, the piano stood in the café, sadly out-of-tune with chipped ivory keys.

Only two of the three parrots who had replaced Polly in 1972 still survived. Polly II was believed to be a male until 1978 when he laid two eggs. Parrots in captivity can lay eggs even if there is no mate present. Polly II's eggs never hatched because they were probably infertile. She died in 1980.

A reporter for the Whitehorse Star wrote in 1985 that, "The outside of the Caribou Hotel is quaint but the bar is dingy, the showers don't work, the lobby is the size of a matchbox and they haven't enough hotel rooms for even one busload of visitors.... That place is not fit for a herd of caribou."

Some of the maintenance had been completed. It was probably during Ray's time that a beam was put under the hotel, apparently not to level it up but to stop it from slumping any deeper.

The wall that had separated men and women in the bar was removed around 1981 and only pillars remained to show where it once stood. The restaurant and bar were further renovated in 1987.

Some of the floors were fixed up in 1985 and the kitchen had work done in 1992.

The third floor had four additional rooms constructed in 1988 and fire escapes were added at each end of the building.

Exactly what happened to the antiques on the third floor and most of the furniture on the second floor is a matter of speculation. They were removed and either sold or disposed of in the early 1990s.

Ray's fix-it efforts paid off and when combined with the management of Alice McGuire, the Caribou became, as one patron described it, "a quaint old pub where a guy could chat with others over a few drinks, maybe play some pool or watch a hockey game."

Ray, already an increasingly frail 90-year-old, was diagnosed with cancer in 1995. His health deteriorated to the point where he couldn't even leave the small shed he lived in behind the hotel. In early 1997, he passed away in the hospital in Whitehorse.

Other than part of the flooring in the bar being replaced in 1999 no further effort was made to repatriate the aging building.

A restored Caribou as a grand hotel had been Ray's vision. The new owner of the Caribou, his son Bob, had no such aspirations.

Chapter 27

MORNING VISITORS

Alice McGuire had been a skeptic before she and her husband Dean took over managing the Caribou in September, 1992.

"Even though I had heard many spirit stories from my grandmother, Jenny LeBarge, and my dad, William Cletheroe, who told us plenty of ghost stories that he experienced," wrote Alice in 2018, "I wasn't a believer until I actually experienced ghostly incidents myself."

Dean, a long-haul trucker, more often than not was on the road so operating the hotel fell exclusively to Alice.

Summer days were long, hard and hectic.

Each morning she awoke before dawn to put on the coffee for the restaurant, start her home baking, and haggle with Rick Halliday, a local commercial fisherman who sold her the fresh lake trout she served at dinner.

When her cook turned up around 8 a.m., she cleaned the bar and headed upstairs to do the housekeeping.

"The rooms were nothing to write home about," she said in 2018, "but I kept them clean and comfortable for the odd tired traveler."

Reverse shadows? Sun and shadow at the top of the stairs resembles a person – except it's the sunny part that resembles a person, not the shadows. According to Anne Morgan, it was a cloudy day and there is nothing at the top of the stairs that could cast shadows to form this image

After lunch she would draw up her list of needed supplies then drive to Whitehorse to pick up groceries and liquor, arriving back just in time to start work.

In the evening she worked in the lounge, usually until she closed it down at two in the morning.

Three or four hours later her day started again.

Winters gave her the opportunity to get some rest.

The restaurant was closed and she didn't rent out any rooms unless there was notice from the WPYR that a crew was going to be in town and needed accommodation.

Only the bar was open for business every day. She had a bartender who turned up at 11 a.m. to open up and Alice herself did the 7 p.m. to 2 a.m. shift.

She allowed herself the luxury of sleeping in until nine every morning and making a leisurely breakfast before spending some time cleaning up the bar and restocking the liquor cabinets and fridge.

Shortly before her bartender was due to arrive she went up to the second floor and drew a hot bath. Then she grabbed a book and sat in the tub, soaking and reading until the water started to get chilly.

It was on October 26, 1993, that the guests first arrived.

Alice was dozing off in the steamy warmth of the bathroom, located across the hall from her suite, when the sound of the lobby door opening awakened her. Then she heard a crowd of people climbing the stairs, laughing and talking.

Alice panicked. The door to her suite was open and she was afraid that whomever it was would go out onto the balcony, which was rickety and rotten and might collapse under their weight. She was wet, naked, and in no position to step out and warn them in time.

She jumped out of the tub and struggled to get into her dressing gown, which stuck to her wet skin at every opportunity.

The people climbing the stairs reached the landing outside the bathroom door.

"So this is what it looks like up here," said a male voice.

Every October 26, Alice McGuire had morning visitors she heard but never saw

A second male voice, "There doesn't seem to be anyone around, what do you think?"

A woman spoke up, "Well, we might as well go back down."

They descended the stairs talking and laughing all the way. Then the lobby door closed and there was silence.

Caribou Hotel ad

By now Alice had managed to get into her dressing gown. She raced down the stairs and into the bar. Her bartender was there alone having a coffee before opening up.

"Why on earth did you let those people go up the stairs?" demanded Alice. The bartender stared at her like she was crazy.

"What are talking about?" she responded. "No one came in here and no one went up the stairs.

I've been here drinking my coffee and I can see both doors. There's nobody around and I didn't hear anyone."

Alice didn't believe her but couldn't think of any reason why she would lie. She settled for cautioning the bartender that if anyone came in and wanted to go upstairs that they shouldn't go onto the balcony.

A meticulous daily diarist, the next time it happened as she went to make her notes she was surprised to realize the visitors turned up on the same day exactly one year later. And again two years later – the same crowd saying the same words while she struggled to get into her dressing gown.

She tried describing it to people but they just laughed at her so she stopped telling the story.

In 1996, a close friend of Alice's, Johanna Tellon, was staying in the hotel.

Alice was in her bath and Johanna was having a shower down the hall. The guests arrived and departed on schedule.

When Alice got out of the bathroom she encountered Johanna coming out of her shower with her head wrapped in a towel.

"Who were all those noisy people and what are they doing up here?" she asked.

"Aha!" shouted Alice, "You heard them too! Those are the spirits I've been trying to tell you about and you didn't believe me."

Johanna looked at her like she was crazy – a look that Alice was now quite used to.

"I'm going downstairs," she told Alice, "and I'm going to get to the bottom of this."

When she came back up the stairs she was puzzled. No one downstairs had seen or heard anything.

"I guess you are telling the truth after all."

Alice was never sure who the spirits were or why they turned up on the same day every year.

"I do know the ocean liner Princess Sophia struck a reef and was lost at sea on the 25th of October, 1918. Perhaps those people are spirits of some of those travelers," she said in 2018. Her first encounter with the mysterious visitors had been 75 years, plus one day, since the sinking of the Princess Sophia.

"So why do I write down my experiences with spirits? I do it because most of the young people in my family don't believe that the soul or spirit in a living person exists. These skeptics, as I once was, believe there is no life after death – which is true – at least not life as we know it. Your soul, your spirit still lives on.

"Why some spirits hang about on earth, after death, is beyond me. Probably because of some mission they haven't completed or just reluctant to leave earth...who knows why. Now I believe my Dad and Grandmother's stories of spirits."

The TV came on by itself, startling both the intruder and his intended victim

Chapter 28

A STRANGER AT MIDNIGHT

While Bessie's activities were mostly benign she could be fiercely protective when it came to what she perceived as threats to her hotel or staff.

When Alice decided to terminate her lease in 1998 she planned to close the hotel on April 2 because Bob Olson's manager would be assuming control of the Caribou on April 3.

On April Fool's Day, her last night for operating the bar, there were only a few customers playing pool and visiting around the wood stove. Alice happened to be watching the pool table when one of the players, Ernie Richard, made what seemed to her to be an impossible pool shot — in which the ball hit the end of the table, bounced up onto the side rail, and ran back toward Ernie before dropping into a pocket and promptly popping out again.

Only Alice and Ernie saw the ball make its improbable journey and as she was describing it to the other patrons she ran her hand along the side rail. She didn't feel any pain but as she lifted her hand from the rail blood shot out from it across the floor. She rushed to the bar, washed her hand, and wrapped a towel around it. Then curious about how badly she had been cut since she still felt no pain, she unwrapped the hand and found

The pool table which Alice retreated behind to protect herself

no injury at all. The other patrons, still cleaning the blood also could find no damage. Neither did they locate any sharp edges along the side of the pool table.

"Now is that a weird incident or not?" she asked in 2018. "I chalked it up to spirits in the hotel who were not very happy about me leaving."

A few years later, for no apparent reason, a third floor window simply blew up — spraying glass all over the sidewalk and street below, fortunately missing the tourists who were there at the time.

"We thought it was Mrs. Gideon," said Carcross resident Daphne Mennell, "who had just had it with the current owner (Bob Olson)."

There were risks to operating a bar in a small town — one of them being alone late at night with no means with which to summon help if it was needed.

In the winter months, when business in the bar was slow, Alice would occasionally shut the doors at midnight rather than waiting until the legal closing time of 2 a.m.

One cold and snowy February night there hadn't been anyone at all in the bar for a couple of hours so she decided to take the rest of the night off. She turned off the kitchen stoves, which she used to prepare food for the bar. The restaurant wasn't open during the winter months so that door was already bolted. She secured the lobby door.

Coming into the bar to turn off the lights and lock up she was startled to see a badly dressed man with long blond hair and a beard standing just inside the front door.

He never said a word but Alice, looking at his piercing blue eyes and grim expression, knew she was in trouble.

"I'm sorry," she said to him, "we're closed," hoping it would be enough to turn him away.

Instead he approached her.

She retreated behind the pool table, trying to keep it between the two of them – all the time telling the man he had to leave, but he didn't respond and kept following her around the table while cutting her off from any doors she might be able to escape through.

Then the television turned on, played for a moment, and turned off. Both of them looked at it.

Alice knew the remote control didn't work. She had been required to manually turn it off earlier in the evening.

The man hesitated, for the first time showing uncertainty in his facial expression. He could see Alice's hands and knew she didn't have a remote control.

It came on again. Louder this time, played a little longer, then turned off. Neither of them moved.

Then a third time, with the volume turned up to a deafening pitch.

"What the hell?" muttered the stranger. He turned and headed for the door.

As he left the hotel Alice moved quickly, slamming the door behind him and jamming the iron security bar across it.

The man stood on the sidewalk in the drifting snow, looking back through the window at Alice for a moment before climbing into a white panel van and driving into the night.

As he vanished the TV turned itself off and there was just silence in the bar.

Alice turned away from the window and sagged against the door.

"Thank you," she said to the empty space, "Thank you, whoever you are."

Caribou Hotel in 2003

Chapter 29

TWO
BOB
OLSONS

You never knew which Bob Olson would show up on any given day.

It might be the hard-working, tenacious National Party candidate who stole the show in an all-candidates forum during the 1993 Canadian Federal Election. His emotional answers and eloquent debating skills apparently skewered his opponents, which included the federal NDP leader Audrey McLaughlin. While the audience had no idea who he was when the evening began and few agreed with his politics, his passion made an impression.

He had no campaign team and virtually no advertising. Realistically, he knew had no chance of winning the election and hoped just to get enough votes to get his deposit back − so felt free to express his opinions rather than recite party platitudes.

With no organization to back him and a national party that couldn't afford to help with expenses Bob was effectively on his own. He covered everything out of his own pocket, driving from town to town to meet with small groups of people and talk about the political landscape of Canada and the Yukon.

Bob Olson

"I don't think I've slept two hours in the past week," he said in an interview midway through the campaign, "But I was a long distance driver. I used to drive 18 to 20 hours, seven days a week. You get used to it."

On voting day he was the only one calling his possible supporters and urging them to get out to vote. Some of them did go to the polling booths but not enough to get his deposit back.

It was his intelligence and dogged determination during the campaign that earned him a small measure of grudging respect from even those Carcross residents who otherwise intensely disliked him.

"He wasn't a stupid man," remembered Alice McGuire, "He was an intelligent man who had an addiction problem and that affected everything he did in his life."

However, even as he showed what he was capable of in the 1993 election there were signs that he had a difficult relationship with the truth. He stated in a 1993 interview with the Yukon News that he had been a steward for Whitehorse United Church for nine years and an executive for the Sourdough Stompers square-dancing club. But there are no records supporting those claims and nobody involved with either organization in the 1980s recalled him at all.

One has to wonder how he even got the nomination to represent the National Party in the Yukon at all since he was living in Vancouver at the time. The campaign literature described him as the long time owner of the Caribou, even though his father Ray actually owned it.

Or you might get the Bob Olson who could be found passed out, sprawled half-naked across his bed in the middle of the day.

His bar manager in the 2000s and friend, Herbert Holstein, later described Bob as "a man without brakes" who drank every day. "At that point in time, I think pretty well anyone could flag him down with a bottle."

Another resident simply called him "a nasty drunk". Yet a third person called the Caribou "a hard-drinking dive".

By the late 1990s people stopped leasing the hotel from him and he had to assume control over the day-to-day operations himself — a job he wasn't capable of doing.

There were reports of nightly fights in the bar, which was described as being "awash in beer and whiskey." Bob didn't care to spend any time trying to curb the violence. He was too busy drinking, trying to chase girls or participating in the scuffle himself. Liquor license violations occurred frequently, usually around serving people already too intoxicated, selling alcohol to underage persons, and public drinking outside the hotel.

As Bob went downhill so did the Caribou. The parrots eventually disappeared and likewise, the tourists who came in to see them. Johnnie Johns died in 1988 and the people who visited him in the Caribou stopped coming. Locals boycotted the place because it was no longer the friendly neighbourhood café and pub it used to be.

What customers still came to the hotel he appreciated in that peculiar manner in which a drunk expresses their love for another drunk. When a fellow drinker died in the hotel, Bob dumped him in the back of his pick-up truck and drove to Whitehorse to deliver the corpse to the morgue. To honour his late patron he kept a candle burning for three days in the front window alongside a glass of beer.

When he could no longer afford to pay a salary to his staff he found employees who were willing to work for free drinks.

The rooms were empty except for those he made available to staff and friends too inebriated to walk or drive home. One customer who came looking for accommodations for the night was told there were no door keys and he could just go upstairs and open the door to any room until he found one he liked.

Upstairs, he found Bob sprawled on his bed, a couple having sex next door, and, in a third room, the furniture supported by the walls because it couldn't stand up on its own any more. He decided not to stay.

Another liked the price of a night's stay — just $10 — but one look at the dilapidated rooms convinced him to keep on going and pay substantially more elsewhere.

There were allegedly drugs being sold in the bar. There were certainly enough incidents of them being used in the immediate vicinity. Many residents blamed Bob for enabling the increasing drug abuse, alcohol addiction, and crime in the community.

The hotel itself became a target for regular break-ins with people shattering the windows after dark and entering the bar looking to score free after-hours booze.

Eventually, Bob moved full-time into the hotel because he couldn't afford to have the liquor walking out the windows in the middle of the night. He sometimes slept on a couch but most nights, after the bar closed, would make up a bed on top of the pool table.

Every once in a while he would stop drinking and the Bob Olson of the 1993 campaign showed up, but those days were increasingly rare and unpredictable.

He became more and more isolated from people and was, according to Herbert, a very unhappy and lonely man.

As he locked the doors after closing early on the morning of December 1, 2004, Bob had already made a decision. The Caribou would never open again — at least not with him as the owner.

The Yukon government had recently made a political and financial commitment to working with the WPYR to bring cruise ship passengers on the railroad from Skagway to Carcross. The return of the train had the potential of turning the small town into the most visited tourist destination in the Yukon and businesses were looking for opportunities to capitalize on it.

It was time to sell.

He had been approached often with offers to purchase the hotel.

Alice and Dean McGuire had an option-to-purchase worked out with Ray but he passed away before it could be exercised. They approached Bob but he wouldn't give them a yes or no or even confirm whether he was going to sell. Finally they gave up, terminated their lease, and walked away from the Caribou in early 1998.

Archie Lang expressed an interest – he and his friend Earl Bennett were regulars at the hotel simply because Archie had never been able to get the Caribou out of his blood after the winter he spent there. Whitehorse businessman Cal Waddington, whose wife Norma had grown up in the Carcross area, came close to finalizing a deal but Bob backed out at the last moment. A contractor from Watson Lake, Jamie Toole and his partner Anne Morgan, communicated with him for at least eight years but those conversations usually got derailed when Bob got "into his cups." And there were others.

On December 15, Whitehorse businessman Norm Jensen got a phone call from Bob.

"I'm going to accept your offer," Bob told him, "How can we close this deal?"

The two men talked a little longer.

"It was a handshake deal. We agreed upon a price and then we decided to meet during the last week of December to work out the details but that never happened. He never made it that far," Norm recalled in 2018. "I intended to restore the building. Build an annex to attract tourists from the buses and trains and serve them lunch. I was going to put a bunch of brass statues out front to remember the legendary owners and patrons of the place. People like Tagish Charlie. Johnnie Johns. Polly. The Gideons. Something that would give people a sense of the history of the place."

The bar where Bob Olson died at Christmas, 2004

Chapter 30

"THE DEVIL MADE ME DO IT"

The body in the snow-filled ditch was unrecognizable but Royal Canadian Mounted Police (RCMP) Constable Elaine Maisonneuve had a pretty good idea who it probably was.

She had just completed delivering gear and sandwiches to other officers searching the area on Monday, December 27, and was slowly cruising down Cronkhite Road in Whitehorse's Wolf Creek sub-division when she spotted tire tracks outside the driving area. Shining her flashlight into the ditch she noticed, "a bonier, fleshier mound of something…. The body was intact except for the facial area which appeared to be scavenged by animals."

She summoned a forensics officer who confirmed it was an adult male. Later, the body was identified by its fingerprints as being that of Bob Olson.

The RCMP had been looking for Bob since that morning. They knew he had been killed and the body dumped in Wolf Creek but were looking in the area where his abandoned truck had been discovered – stuck in the ditch on Langholz Road. The truck contained a caribou head, some picture frames, a blood-soaked pillow and some bloodied work gloves.

Residents told the RCMP they hadn't seen anybody but the truck had been there since Christmas Eve.

Herbert Holstein was the first to realize something had gone seriously wrong late on the afternoon of December 24. Two brothers stopped by his house to tell him the doors of the Caribou were wide open to the elements, there were no lights on, and the bar area was in disarray.

Herbert entered the hotel and looked inside the bar. On the pool table Bob's bed lay undisturbed just as he made it up each night. Chairs were knocked over. There was shattered glass on and behind the bar and on the floor was a pool of blood. The woodstove was cold. There obviously hadn't been a fire in it all day and standing water in one of the sinks had frozen over.

He called RCMP Constable Jeffrey Kalles who turned up a few minutes later.

"You check the rooms upstairs. See if Bob is up there," Jeffrey told Herbert, "but don't go into the bar."

The Constable noted the pool of blood Herbert had seen had a footprint in. He also found blood in a garbage can and spattered on some furniture. Later, a pair of glasses were found and pieces of Bob's dentures. Standing undamaged in the midst of the shattered glass was a lone Tequila bottle.

Looking around the outside of the hotel the officer realized Bob's truck was missing.

"I felt that Mr. Olson was either hurt or needed assistance," he testified in the trial in 2006. Once he secured the bar area he contacted the Whitehorse detachment and put out a watch for Bob and his truck – a black pickup with a red stripe down the side.

About the same time, on December 27, that the truck was found, Bob's nephew Dean Boucher turned himself into the RCMP in Whitehorse. His uncle was dead, he told the police. He and a friend, Mark Lange, had dumped his body in Wolf Creek but couldn't remember exactly where. Mark turned himself in three days later.

The end of the day on December 23, a Thursday, was a cold and windy night. There had been a light rain on Wednesday so the ground was slick with ice. Dean and Mark had been drinking and were walking across the narrows on the railroad bridge. Jeffrey Kalles, the only RCMP in Carcross that day, spotted them and stopped them thinking one of them might be a runaway youth he was searching for.

He talked with Boucher, whom he recognized, but decided not to have a long conversation because Dean was obviously upset and angry about something. He asked Mark, whom he didn't know, what he was doing in Carcross. Mark didn't want to talk to him either so he drove away to continue his search.

The last time he saw the two men they were standing beside Bob's truck, which was parked in front of the Caribou.

Even though the bar was closed Bob let Mark and Dean into the hotel.

It had been an unusual day for Bob. The toxicology done during the autopsy on his body showed he was stone-cold sober. He hadn't had a drink or used a drug all day. He had just finished making his bed on the pool table.

Events got more convoluted after the two men entered the bar.

In one version of the story, Dean was pouring drinks at the bar when Mark started beating Bob. They had been arguing over Bob's truck, which Mark wanted to borrow to drive to Whitehorse and buy drugs.

"(He) just attacked him, jumped him," said Dean. Mark already had a criminal record for assault from 1996 when he and a group of friends had kicked in a man's door and beat him in his home. He had also been convicted for spousal assault that same year.

In another version, it was Dean who started beating Bob because the hotel owner refused to give him a piece of art hanging on the wall in the bar.

"(Boucher) attacked out of the blue and started robbing the place," claimed Mark, who admitted that he had joined in late and held Bob down while Dean battered him.

And yet a third story, where Bob threw Mark out of the hotel and started giving Dean a lecture. Dean was known to be "light-fingered" and "always looking for something else to steal." He was also an alcoholic and drug addict but to this point didn't have a record of violence.

Wreath commemorating Bob Olson still hung on the hotel wall in 2006

"He started giving me shit," said Dean. He told me I had a beautiful family and what the fuck was wrong with me. That I was nothing but a punk and a fucking loser.... I had drank a bottle of whiskey to myself, on top of beers all day. I don't know what I did. I don't know how bad I beat him. Mark had nothing to do with the fight at all.... I'm two different people when I'm drunk. I don't know what I'm capable of when I'm in blackouts."

During the trial in 2006, the crown prosecutor presented evidence that both men participated in the assault but didn't really try to clarify the conflicting accounts.

"Your Lordship does not have to decide who inflicted the fatal blow," said Crown attorney Edith Campbell to the presiding judge, "because they were acting together."

Whatever the reason for the attack Bob was beaten with fists, battered by a telephone Dean ripped off the wall, football kicked to a pulp then left fatally wounded on the floor of the bar.

The two men stripped some artwork off the walls, stole what cash they could find, took a bunch of beer and loaded it into the truck. Then they picked up Bob, apparently still alive at the time, and tossed him into the back of his truck. For some reason, they covered him with a jacket and put a pillow under his head. They drove to Wolf Creek and dumped him into a ditch. While escaping the two accidently drove off the road and got the truck mired in the snow.

A few hours later, sometime before 4 a.m. on December 24, Michael Wren, the owner of a gas station at a nearby small industrial area named McCrae, was surprised to see Dean and Mark walk out of the cold night to tell him they were stuck and could he give them a tow.

Dean, he said, was so agitated that he was physically shaking. When he leaned on the counter in the store, "I could feel the actual counter rocking, sort of a rhythmic motion."

He suggested they call another company to get the tow but they decided to call a taxi instead.

While waiting for the taxi Dean told Michael, "The devil made me do it" but declined to say what the devil made him do.

Dean and Mark were convicted of second-degree murder in 2006. Upon appeal, they were granted a new trial in 2011 and pled guilty to manslaughter.

Jamie Toole and Anne Morgan on the day they took possession of the hotel

Chapter 31

RESTORATION

A few months after Bob Olson's death, his sister Lorraine, the executor of the estate, phoned Norm Jensen and asked if he still wanted to buy the hotel. Apparently, Bob had made note of the "handshake deal" he and Norm had reached.

"No," replied Norm, "I don't think so." He felt a little weird about buying a place where a murder had just occurred.

Then Jamie Toole and Anne Morgan showed Bob's sister eight years of letters and faxes which detailed the talks they had had with Bob. She gave them first right of refusal – just in time, because a week later the WPYR expressed an interest.

It took another 18 months for the estate to be settled but in 2006 ownership of the hotel transferred to Jamie and Anne.

They knew the building wasn't in great shape but their first detailed investigation of the structure was almost too much.

The hotel was simply sitting on the ground. If there had ever been a foundation under it, it had long ago rotted away and or sunk into the sand. The only thing stopping the hotel from folding up into itself like a deck of cards was a single unsupported centre beam that had probably been put in by Ray Olson. There was a shallow crawl space underneath with a floor of loose sand and pipes and wires of every size, shape, and era hanging down.

"You were almost risking your life just to crawl under there," said Anne.

On the surface, the back wall looked well weathered but solid. Jamie wasn't convinced it was what it appeared to be. The hotel tilted severely toward the back (when they measured there was over a half metre – just under a two foot-difference between the front and back of the floor). There were no gutters along the roofline to drain the rain and water from melting snow away from the building. It had to have run down the back wall and some, if not most of it, had likely seeped down inside the wall.

He pushed his hand through the wallboard, which turned out to be almost as thin as a piece of paper with not much on the other side. Closing his fingers, he pulled a fistful of rotten wood out of the hole.

There had been some repairs done to the wall with what turned out to be materials cannibalised from the hotel's original bar but those were mostly cosmetic.

The floor beneath his feet wasn't in any better condition. He was able to push his hand through the boards and pull mouldy, punky wood from there as well.

As they walked through the hotel rooms on the second and third floor they peeled back some of the wall material around the light switches and electrical outlets. Every fixture had a charred area around it. There was not a room in the place, Jamie realized, that hadn't had an undetected electrical flash in it. The hotel had indeed led a charmed life, they now understood, to have survived this long.

Behind the hotel they discovered two sheds stuffed full with paint thinner, old gasoline cans, aerosols, and cases of empty beer bottles.

"It stunk and it was rotten and it was so flammable I can't believe it didn't just blow up on its own," said Anne.

She recalled standing behind the hotel thinking, "I love old stuff. I love the history. I just wanted to run a bed and breakfast...but this!? Oh my God.

Digging out the crawl space under the hotel in 2007

What have we done?"

Jamie, standing beside her, had his own thoughts. "This is Anne's dream. If she couldn't have found a historical building in the Yukon (to purchase and renovate), she was going to move back to Victoria.... I could either leave Anne or figure out how to do this."

Top priority was raising the existing structure and putting a proper foundation under the building. It was one of those "easier said than done" items.

The back wall had to be entirely rebuilt first or it would disintegrate under the stress.

The interior had to be totally gutted to reduce the weight of the building and make the structure more flexible because while being hiked up the building also had to be levelled. It had taken a long time to become crooked. The wood had slowly adjusted to its off-kilter shape and was brittle with age. There was a risk the building might literally explode if raised and levelled too quickly.

There had to be a solid temporary frame on which the hotel would sit while a permanent foundation was built under it.

Room interiors on the second floor before renovations

When the lift happened it was a nerve-wracking day.

"It was terrifying," Anne recalled, "It was like gunshots going off in here. There was a gale blowing and you could see right outside through the cracks in the wall."

Despite the racket nothing exploded the day they jacked up the hotel. Two beams did blow apart when the building was resettled on the permanent foundation in 2008. They replaced the beams with metal ones.

The main floor and second floor levelled off perfectly. The third floor didn't.

"Somewhere all the crookedness had to stop and it stopped on the third floor," said Jamie. "It's still crooked but you can't feel it and you can't see it with the naked eye.

"When we bought the hotel it was already in danger of collapsing in on itself. If we hadn't built the foundation and the back wall I think that within five years this place would have become a pile of rubble on the ground all by itself. I don't think anyone else would have done what we have to the hotel. Not that anyone else couldn't have done it, they probably just wouldn't have."

Modern conveniences were added. In-floor heating replaced the wood-burning stove in the bar. Initially, they operated the heating system off a high-efficiency furnace in the basement but the plumbing system has since been modified to operate on geothermal heat. A well was drilled under the hotel and produced sufficient energy to heat the hotel when hooked up. All of it hidden beneath a veneer of 1910 decor.

"It'll look old on the surface," Jamie said, "but there's the heating system and in the walls there is Wi-Fi, security, and fire suppression. It will be high-tech modern — just like it was a technological marvel when they built it in 1910."

The roof was repaired. Windows replaced. New electrical wiring installed. Additional layers of insulation were added, the siding replaced and painted battleship gray. The old kitchen was converted into a walk-in cooler. The metal clad siding on the walk-in cooler and the cooler itself were the last remaining vestiges of the Yukon Hotel from Bennett.

In 2018, the hotel was still closed.

"People keep asking us, 'Why isn't it open yet?'" said Anne. "I don't think they realize how much work had to go into this to make it safe, efficient, and ready to be opened. We've done this much and there's still more to do.... And it's terribly expensive. Once we got started on this we had no choice but to go all out. Historically, we had to do it right, not cheap our way through it or it wouldn't be right."

She traveled to antique dealers across Canada and the United States, seeking out period furniture and fixtures because there was nothing left in the hotel when they bought it.

The couple knew the history of each piece they acquired. The "new" bar is made of old doors from churches in England. You can have a religious ceremony then order a beer without leaving the room.

Anne was able to salvage the piano pulled out of the hotel fire in 1909, an old poker table and cash register from the bar, a hotel safe, Polly's original cage, and some claw-foot bathtubs dating back to the Gideons.

There was more history hidden under the floor and in the walls of the Caribou.

Jamie and Anne spent a week crawling on their bellies in the cramped space under the hotel, digging with shovels, and hauling sand out in buckets. Buried in the sand they discovered a woodstove that came from the original hotel before it burned in 1910, melted glass and old coal oil lantern brackets in addition to a two-metre (six-foot) section of the original bar.

When ripping out the walls in preparation for the lifting of the building they found a Toronto Star Weekly newspaper with the front-page headline announcing the sinking of the Lusitania in May, 1915. There was a Mumm's champagne bottle somehow jammed inside a wall on the second floor. Another wall revealed a medicine bottle. The medication, Merz Santal, was apparently considered the aspirin of its day and recommends the user to not "exceed 10-12 capsules per day or as directed by a physician." When removing some buffalo board – a thick cardboard composite interior siding the US Army had installed on the walls on the main floor – a menu from the mess hall used by construction crews building the Alaska Highway was discovered tacked to the wall underneath.

Jamie in the bar with a vintage cash register during renovations in 2016

Gooderham & Worts Rye Whiskey bottles. One found under a step in the stairwell and the other purchased from the liquor store in Whitehorse in 2007

When working on the stairs Jamie discovered a whiskey bottle in one of the cavities under the steps. The label read "Gooderham and Worts Rye Whiskey." One morning, when Jamie and Anne were in Toronto, Ontario, for a short holiday they discovered a plaque which told them the B&B they were staying in was the former location of the offices for Gooderham and Worts. The company had distilled whiskey under its own name from 1837 until 1926 when it was bought out and absorbed by Hiram Walker and Sons Distillery. At its peak, Gooderham and Worts produced 25% of all whiskey distilled in Canada.

"The Gideons used to have a bit of a museum of gold rush artefacts in the hotel," Anne decided, "So we'll do the same, only with artefacts of Carcross history and the hotel's history instead of the Klondike Gold Rush."

Notice of Designation of Historic Site

January 25, 2008
Pursuant to Section 19 of the *Historic Resources Act*

Caribou Hotel

Lot Two (2), Block A
Plan 67560
Carcross, Yukon Territory

Is designated a Yukon Historic Site

Elaine Taylor
Minister

Yukon
Tourism and Culture

Chapter 32

HISTORY SELLS

Carcross overflows with history and of all the buildings in town the Caribou is the iconic landmark most representative of the community's connection to its past.

The downtown core consists of three weathered buildings all rebuilt after the 1909 fire: the Caribou, Mathew Watson's Store, and the White Pass train depot.

Along the beach facing out to Bennett Lake and scattered around the community on both sides of the narrows are notable older homes and businesses, many transported to the community from Whitehorse and vanished towns like Conrad and Bennett. Others, such as the house built by Colonel Conrad and used to house guests by the Gideons following the fire of 1909, still stand on their original sites.

Scattered across the landscape in front of the hotel – all of them visible from the balcony over the main entry – are the miniature train engine from the Taku Tram, the Duchess, an old open stagecoach once used to deliver the Royal Mail, the memorialized remnants of the Tutshi, which was torched by an arsonist and mostly burned in 1990, and a replica of Skookum Jim's house.

The spot where the golden spike was driven to finish the WPYR in 1900 is just below the balcony and the train swing bridge can also be seen. The railroad is listed as an "International Historic Civil Engineering Landmark" – the same accolade accorded to the Eiffel Tower and Statue of Liberty.

However, when you study tourists' photographs the most common image captured is the hotel. Even shuttered it is an object of curiosity.

When a photo of the hotel as it is today appears in a magazine or on a website there is invariably someone commenting on it, telling of their experience or sending a photo showing the hotel as being black with white trim – which was how it was painted during much of Dorothy Hopcott's tenure.

The awe-inspiring snow-capped mountains, clear water lakes, and lush valleys surrounding Carcross also come with history that reaches back millennia.

In 1997, two sheep hunters approached a patch of ice on the side of a mountain just north of Carcross. They noticed a thick black material near the edge of the melting ice and could smell something that made them think of manure from a farmyard. It was caribou dung, but in amounts

Caribou on Ice Patch

Caribou sculpture greets visitors to Carcross

never seen before that bore witness to the First Nation legends of massive herds covering the mountainsides.

Further investigation uncovered a wooden hunting dart, which apparently had just melted out of the ice and turned out to be 4,300 years old. It is one of Canada's most ancient artefacts built from an organic material. The dung itself was tested at 2,400 years of age.

The Yukon Ice Patch Project was born as a result of that discovery and scientists visited similar ice patches on other mountains, discovering over 200 artefacts preserved in the ice for thousands of years that were only now melting out because of climate change and a string of hot summers in the late 1990s.

The findings told a history of generations of hunters hunting first with spears, then darts thrown from a throwing board (called an atlatl), and finally bows and arrows – with blades made of bone, antler, stone, and native copper. If the projectile missed its mark it might disappear in the ice and snow. Because ice patches don't move like glaciers the artefacts didn't get crushed and broken beyond recognition. Instead they were frozen in time, preserved in almost the same condition as they were when lost.

Other artefacts included animal bones, preserved animal tissue, hides, and feathers that helped to identify the prehistoric prey – mostly birds, sheep, bison, and caribou.

Caribou still seek out ice patches in the mountains in summer. It provides them with relief from clouds of annoying insects and escape from the heat. Knowing the herds could reliably be found on the ice patches made them a good place for hunters to get close.

Ice Patch archaeology became a scientific specialty in its own right. The idea spread from the Yukon and similar finds have since been located in Alaska, British Columbia, the Northwest Territories, Colorado, and Norway. The Yukon Ice Patches have been nominated as a UNESCO World Heritage Site.

More recent mountain top history includes abandoned mines, the roads and tramlines leading to them and ruins of small towns. Then there are the unspoiled places where the animal and plant kingdoms still hold sway.

Some writers and historians believe people are closeted in their urban environments where older homes are dismantled in favour of "monster houses" or condos. The charm of the corner grocer is being replaced by the barren environment of a big box store. People are losing their connection to the past and unspoiled nature and how they validate the present.

For them words like "Never Again" and "Lest We Forget" are losing their power to influence the future. Unspoiled nature is a postage stamp of green in the midst of urban sprawl. Peace and solitude are no longer to be sought in the noisy solitude of the wilderness but behind a set of headphones or ear buds relaying the imitated hush of the wind through branches or the crash of waves on a stony shore.

That loss, they believe, diminishes people spiritually and impoverishes us socially.

Regaining what is being lost is possibly the reason so many history tourists and eco-tourists seek out places like Skagway and Carcross with their abundance of antiquities and natural grandeur.

It is why when confronted with Carcross Common, a cultural retail and coffee complex built in 2012, visitors are just as curious about Carcross's quirky main street and its stories of historical legends and events as they are about shopping.

In 2016, in excess of 100,000 visitors passed through Carcross during its three-month summer season – making it the most visited community in the Yukon. Approximately 10% of the cruise ships passengers who arrive in Skagway each year made the trip on the train, by bus or drive a jeep to Carcross. The WPYR added Carcross back onto its list of destinations on the railroad in 2006.

Heritage Yukon, a society formed in 1976 to support individuals and groups interested in preserving the Yukon's past, set its sights on Carcross in 1978.

"Carcross needs protection," said society chairman Rolf Hougen of Whitehorse, "as the town as a whole is not protected. I believe it has great potential." Carcross, he noted, was near the top of a historical priority list in a study conducted by the Yukon Government in 1974.

A project of the type needed in Carcross, Rolf added, could be legislated by the government but in the end it would be the people of Carcross who would have to do the work.

A development plan was created in the late 1970s but it would be another 20 years before work on preserving Carcross began in earnest. Since 2000 the waterfront area has had a boardwalk constructed to the dock. The warehouse on the dock was renovated to be potentially turned into a commercial space and the shaky, derelict footbridge across the narrows was replaced with a modern more stable version. The burned hulk of the Tutshi was memorialized.

Carcross Common was constructed because, according to the Carcross/ Tagish Management Corporation's chief executive officer Justin Ferbey, Carcross had little to offer visitors when they arrived.

They arrive in town to use the washroom and buy ice cream then they're gone, he said in a series of interviews in 2012. While the retail village might not necessarily convince them to stay longer, it would give them something more to do while they are there "and it will work only if the product is valuable, if it's unique, looks nice, and it is community and First Nations driven.

"The challenge is the cost of building in Carcross is the same as Whitehorse, but rent is nowhere near what it is in Whitehorse, so you don't have a great financial return...every investment is always a risk and Carcross is hugely risky. But you don't get a return without a risk."

The Common included coffee shops, craft shops, an information centre, and a master carvers' studio.

Historical tourism isn't limited to just Carcross. In 2016, the Carcross/Tagish First Nation started building a frontier hotel on the location of Friedrich Trump's Arctic Hotel in Bennett. The idea was to lure tourists to the abandoned town, which has only one original building, St. Andrew's Church, still standing and only one permanent resident. The new Arctic Hotel consisted of four canvas tents of the type used by prospectors and miners during the gold rush, furnished with antique beds and carpets.

It was part of an interpretive tour of the town site, a destination for eco-tourists, and possibly rooms in which hikers could stay after retracing the steps of Tlingit and Tagish traders and Klondike Gold stampeders over the Chilkoot Trail.

While the ultimate goal was to make Carcross a destination – like it had been in the days of Johnnie Johns – rather than merely a stop on the road to somewhere else, a large part of the development came about because there was no economy in Carcross.

The community had one of the highest rates of unemployment in the Yukon and young people were leaving because they could see no reason to stay.

The elders were despairing because, while there had been many large projects and events in Carcross's history, none of them left a lasting legacy that could be passed onto the next generations. There had been plenty of debate over development plans or the lack of them but, as Crag Lake resident Gisela Niedermeyer stated, "living in a town as poor as Carcross, people are more worried about putting food on the table than coming to a meeting."

"You go to Carcross today and every single summer and every single winter, people are saying, 'What employment opportunities are there for young people?'" said management corporation CEO Justin Ferbey in 2014, "And the answer, outside of working as a bureaucrat for the government, is 'zero'."

There was one exception to his statement.

In 2012, documentary filmmaker Kelly Milner purchased a cabin near the foot of Montana Mountain on the south side of the narrows. Every morning she watched a line of teenagers from Carcross shoulder tools, march across the footbridge, and disappear into the road leading up the mountain.

"They were like the seven dwarfs going off to work," she said and they tweaked her interest.

The program, she discovered, was called Single Track to Success and it had already made Carcross a destination. Above her cabin, hidden in the forest and reaching above tree line almost to the top of the mountain were 65 kilometres (43 miles) of what was considered some of the best mountain biking trails in the world. They were attracting almost 4,000 riders a year from across Canada, the United States, Europe, and Asia.

The line of teenagers that caught her eye was the trail crew, heading off each morning to build new trails and improve the old ones.

The idea started with Wayne Roberts, an adventure tourism employee, who started improving an old trail through the bush on Montana Mountain in 1999 on which to take his customers for rides.

Eventually somebody at the Carcross/Tagish First Nation noticed and realized there was potential there that needed to be developed. Jane Keopke, a Whitehorse-based consultant, was contacted in 2004 and asked to put together a business plan for them.

Three months later, after scouring the side of the mountain with Carcross elders searching for potential routes, researching the mountain biking industry (there were 40 million mountain bikes sold in North America in 2010), and arranging a partnership with Vancouver, BC's Capilano College Mountain Bike Operations Program, she founded Single Track to Success.

Graduates from Capilano College taught the local youth how to construct mountain bike trails, mark them properly, and maintain them. They started with the trail cut in 1999 by Wayne Roberts and expanded from there.

Single Track to Success addressed the issue of youth unemployment,

Jamie, Anne and the Frantic Follies cast behind the scenes of CBC Television's Dragon's Den in Toronto, Ontario, 2013

added a new dimension to the Carcross economy, and introduced a healthier lifestyle for the community.

When he was cutting trails, recalled Wayne Roberts in 2012, people in Carcross were upset. They thought it would interfere with hunting and wildlife. Today, he said, the same people were asking him if their kids could be part of the crew and "suddenly I'm seeing older people riding around town on mountain bikes."

Justin told the story of a potential trail crew employee turning up for her job interview in 2013. She was exhausted and he wondered if she was capable of doing the work.

"You seem to be out of breath with the office only on the second floor," he said to her.

"Sorry," she replied breathlessly, "I just got chased by a bear for a kilometre."

He hired her without the interview.

Crew members grew as individuals while working on the mountain, consultant Jane Keopke noted in 2016. The criteria for being a part of the tail crew right from the beginning wasn't necessarily how fit the person was but how much of a desire to work hard they had.

"They're receiving a foundation of incredibly hard work ethic that will set them up for success in whatever they chose to do in life."

In 2013, Single Track to Success was nominated for the Tourism Industry Association of Canada's Innovator of the Year Award. Its nomination was unique in that it pitted a group of 16-year-old northern First Nations' youth who worked with hand tools against engineers, scientists, and business executives from fancy resorts and sophisticated projects in eastern Canada.

One of the trails on Montana Mountain, named Mountain Hero, was inducted into the International Mountain Biking Association's elite Epic Trails' category.

"To me," said Wayne Roberts upon hearing of the designation, "I just won the Nobel Prize for trail building."

Outside magazine – the largest adventure publication in the United States – named Carcross as the world's best destination for mountain biking.

Art House was part of the development to make Carcross more visitor friendly in the 2010s

When the Duke and Duchess of Cambridge, William and Kate, visited Carcross in 2016 one of their activities was an event honouring the youth involved in Single Track to Success.

In 2018, the WPYR was sold to the world's largest leisure travel company, Carnival Corporation, which operated three cruise lines (Carnival, Holland America and Princess Tours) that made regular visits to Skagway. The purchase ensured the railway would continue as a shore excursion for most of the million or so passengers who visited Skagway each year, potentially inflating the numbers who made the longer trip to Carcross.

Yet, even as all this development was going on in the town there was one drawback — beyond a few bed and breakfast places, there were no accommodations in the town. The management corporation considered building a motel but, given their close proximity to Whitehorse, determined the plan wasn't financially feasible.

Which left only the still-shuttered Caribou and its ongoing renovations.

Initially, Jamie and Anne received a federal grant to help with the work and invested a great deal of their own savings. However, the project was massively expensive because of their insistence that original material had to be reworked, refinished, and reused where it could be and the pot of money eventually dried up.

The work slowed to a crawl because both owners had to work full-time at their respective careers to pay as they went: Anne as executive director of the Recreation and Parks Association of the Yukon (RPAY) in Whitehorse and Jamie as a building contractor in Watson Lake.

They courted other funding sources.

In 2013, they were auditioned for and selected to make a pitch to business executives looking for investment opportunities on CBC television's Dragon's Den. They turned up in the Toronto, Ontario, TV studio with a stuffed parrot that could talk and a musical entourage in tow. Grant Simpson, co-owner of Whitehorse's internationally known Frantic Follies had written original music for the performance. He hammered ragtime out of a piano while his business partner Lyall Murdoch played a saw like a violin and two members of their company danced the cancan.

"I don't think the Dragons had ever seen legs like that before," remembered Anne. "They were just astounded by the talent of those two girls." Some of the executives were interested but they came up $50,000 short of making an investment despite being exhorted by one Dragon influenced by consuming a few too many Ice Worm Cocktails.

The hotel itself did host one major party even though it was still closed. The Canadian Parks and Recreation Association held their annual meeting in Whitehorse and asked Anne if she could host a wrap-up celebration in the Caribou. Once again the Frantic Follies provided the music and by the end of the night "the whole building was shaking," Anne said. "I went downstairs because I was nervous. I watched the wood flex and bend under the dancing and I'm not a church person but I prayed, 'God. I hope that floor doesn't collapse.'"

It was designated as a territorial historical landmark building in 2008. In 2010, they received the Yukon Historical and Museums Association's Heritage Conservation Project of the Year Award.

In the meantime they plugged along, spending the money when they could afford it and doing the work when they had the time. Each year, they hoped they might have one part of the hotel, the bar where they could serve food and drinks at lunch, open for business for the following tourist season. And each year, they were disappointed.

One afternoon in 2017 Anne looked around the café area. The sign from the roof sat on sawhorses in the restaurant. They were rehabilitating it to withstand another century of being sandblasted by the prevailing winds and sand dunes of the beach on Bennett Lake. A small part of the original bar, already refinished, stood in one corner waiting to be installed. Stacks of old, refinished, and new wood littered the floor and counters. Tools filled the gaps between the stacks of wood.

In the bar she could see the pressed metal tiles they had painstakingly replaced on the ceiling. Around her were exposed walls that had been insulated with old newspapers, waiting to be reinsulated and reboarded. Remnants of the lathe board hung by W.H. Smith in 1910 could be seen on unfinished interior walls.

"It's a whole lot of hard work," she sighed wearily, "We spend every hour we can in here or looking for furniture to put in here. But we don't regret any of it. It's become a labour of love."

Chapter 33

"SHE'S STILL RUNNING THE HOTEL"

"We didn't know it was haunted when we bought it," Anne said with a smile, "But we're pretty aware of it now."

Early on they noticed that some local residents tended to avoid the hotel but she and Jamie weren't sure why. Then they started to hear the stories.

Employees at the visitor reception centre in the White Pass train depot reported looking up and seeing someone or something standing in the corner window gazing out at them. Sometimes she might be by herself. Other times, witnesses swore, she had what looked like a parrot perched on her shoulder. Photos reveal that only two women, Bessie Gideon and Louise Alexander, were able to successfully pose with Polly perched on their shoulder.

Others noticed Bessie moving back and forth like she was sitting in a rocking chair. Sometimes even ghosts apparently need to get off their tired feet.

There was Archie Lang's story of Mrs. Gideon's visit. Dorothy Hopcott and Don McLellan were visited by her in the same second-floor suite. Other

Of course, there was the explanation for the plywood, which closed off access to the stairs leading up from the second floor.

Dorothy had bumped into someone or something up there. It was why the staircase was blocked off. According to June Tooley, her husband Pat and brother-in-law Gerry, who operated the bar in the early 1990s, talked about meeting Mrs. Gideon on the top floor.

Both Anne and Jamie thought it was cool to own a "haunted" hotel although they held onto a healthy amount of scepticism.

The idea of a haunting didn't help gain credibility when Jamie and a friend were sitting in the bar and noticed a young couple on the street pointing at the hotel, then heading hesitantly toward the front window so they could peek inside. The two men in the bar crouched down and scurried over to hunch down below the windowsill. When the couple were peering through the window they leapt up in front of them.

"It was hilarious," remembered Jamie, "They jumped back, almost fell off the sidewalk, then the girl started laughing and she couldn't stop."

It was that type of antic that ghostly legends are made of he thought.

Then it started happening to them.

Shortly after they purchased the hotel in 2006 and before they started any renovation work, Anne was in Carcross for a meeting of swimming pool managers.

"How come the lights are on in the hotel?" she was asked by one of the people at the meeting.

"What are you talking about?" responded Anne, "There are no lights on in the hotel. There's no power to the building."

"No, the third floor!" chimed in another individual, "There's lights on in there."

"There's no lights on in the hotel," insisted Anne, positive they were pulling her leg. "You're full of baloney."

However, they persisted, even pointing out the window where they had seen the light. It was the corner window. The room that had been Millie McMurphy's playroom in 1939 and the same one that Bessie had been seen frequenting since 1933.

In 2015, shortly after the stamp from Canada Post was released to commemorate the haunting of the Caribou, Jannette Corby — Louise Dawson's granddaughter and Bessie Gideon's grandniece — came to the Yukon to visit a friend in Whitehorse.

Jannette's friend was ill the day they planned to drive to Carcross so she turned up at the Caribou by herself. Anne met her and took her on a tour of the lower floor.

"I'd really like to show you the second floor where Mrs. Gideon lived," said Anne at the end of the tour.

"Yes. I would like to see that."

Jamie had closed off the stairs to the second floor to stop people from wandering into a construction zone so Anne went back into the café to find a screwdriver with which to remove the barricade. As she hunted around for the tool she heard Jannette calling up the stairs.

"Hi Bessie. Hi Mrs. Gideon," Jannette said, "I'm your grand-niece and I live in California. Don Corby is my dad. He used to live in the hotel and has lots of memories."

Then, just as Anne located the screwdriver she needed, there was silence. When she walked into the entryway at the bottom of the stairs, Jannette looked as if she'd seen a ghost.

"What's wrong?!" Anne asked, "What happened?!"

"I was talking to her," replied Jannette in a shaky voice, "I was talking to her up the stairs...and she answered me. I'M NOT KIDDING! Mrs. Gideon banged on the wall, like this." She pounded her fist against a large box mounted on the wall beside her, "She knocked three times."

Then pulling herself together, she looked up the stairs and glanced at Anne.

"I'm not going up there."

"Are you sure? I don't have any problem showing you the second floor."

"I'm not going up there. You cannot convince me to go up there."

With that she marched to the door and left the hotel with Anne following in her wake, still carrying the screwdriver.

In 2015, web-streaming paranormal documentary makers Neil Macdonald and Dave Hamelin had just completed recording a segment on Bessie Gideon at the Caribou. Neil, working alone in one room, silently thanked the ghosts for allowing them to work in the hotel. Suddenly he felt a cold shiver run up his spine. It was like there was someone behind him, Neil said, and whomever it was had malicious intent. He walked out without turning around.

Dave was viewing rough footage from the day's shoot on his computer when he noticed an odd refraction of light in one of the windows.

"We saw some weird light bending in one of the windows that seemed unnatural, but the sun was on the other side (of the building). It almost looked like someone was standing in the window."

The show, Yukon Paranormal, streamed the Bessie Gideon segment in January, 2016.

"She's still running the hotel," concluded Anne in 2017.

When they re-opened the hotel in 2019 she believed Mrs. Gideon was there with them.

There was a bell in the bar for people to ring if they wanted to buy a round for the house.

The first ring of the bell wasn't a round for the house.

It was a toast to the ghost.

Holly Ferguson looks out the third floor window said to be used frequently by Mrs. Gideon's ghost

ACKNOWLEDGMENTS

My thanks in particular to Anne Morgan, Jamie Toole, and the Yukon Historic Resources Fund for their support in writing this story.

Anne's passion for knowledge about the Caribou was very much a reason for uncovering the story told within.

I would like to acknowledge the traditional knowledge of the Carcross/Tagish First Nation shared via such stories as Game Mother.

My appreciation also to the following people who willingly gave interviews or provided stories to myself and Anne or provided resources, references and/or permissions so I could complete this work. If there is any person or source I missed, I take full responsibility and apologize for my error.

Charles Harrison. June Tooley. Sam Holloway. Harry Kern. Millie Jones (McMurphy). Dorothy Hopcott (deceased). Don McLellan (deceased). Annie Auston. Dorothy Gibson. Hollie Smith. Tim Keopke. Michael Gates. Roberta Auston. Archie Lang. Murray Lundberg. Norm Jensen. Clarence Craig (deceased). Arthur Mitchell. Fred Smith. Donna Clayson. Chris Ross. Willie Ross. Harlan Moen. Cheryl Davidson. Larry McLellan. Alice McGuire. Willard Phelps. Nancy Firth (deceased). Dennis and Christine McClure. Vivian Belik at Yukon Archives. Karl Gurcke at US National Parks Service. Michael Nore. Daphne Mennell. Janette Corby. Aubyn Coad. Jane Ferguson. Ken Coates. Canada Post

A good editor always makes a book better. Thank you Erin McMullan.

BIBLIOGRAPHY

Online resources

21ghosts.info/Yukon, 93regimentalcan.com, alaskahighwayarchives.ca, atlinhistory.com, canadianmysteries.ca, caribouhotel.ca, eco.gov. yk.ca, ExploreNorth.com, growthservicesgroup. com, Hougen Group (Yukon Nuggets by Les McLaughlin), Moccasin Telegraph, newspapers. com, ojs.library.ubc.ca, parkscanada.gc.ca (Chilkoot Trail National Historic Site), Steamboats.org, worldisround.com, YouTube, YukonAlaska.com, yukonhistoricplaces.ca, Yukon Paranormal (YouTube).

Newspapers, magazines, news media

The Bennett Sun, Calgary Herald, Canada Post news release, Canadian Home Journal, The Carcross Chronicle, CBC News, CBC North, CKRW, CNN, Cottage Life Magazine, Global News, Maclean's Magazine, National Post, Northern Times, The Alaska Daily Empire, The Atlantic, The Guardian, Up Here Magazine, What's Up Yukon, Whitehorse Daily Star, Yukon Historical & Museums Association Newsletter, Yukon Howl, Yukon News, Yukon Reader, Yukon Sun, Yukoner Magazine.

Unpublished resources

Hollie Smith. Evolution of a Scallywag, Reginald Brooks. History of Engineer Mine, Amanda Frotten's 2016 speech as a Yukon Sourdough Rendezvous Queen candidate.

Books, booklets, pamphlets, theses

Batten, John H. The Forest and The Plain. Clinton: Amwell Press, Clinton, 1984.

Bennett Walking Tour and Bennett Historic Adventure, White Pass & Yukon Route.

Big Game Hunting in Yukon Territory, hunting brochure for Johnnie Johns.

Cameron, Charlotte. A Cheechako in Alaska and Yukon. T. Fisher Unwin Ltd, 1920

Carcross Historic Buildings walking tour, Government of Yukon.

Carr, Emily. Sister and I in Alaska. Vancouver: Figure 1 Publishing, 2014.

Carson, Brenda E., et al. Carcross Region Heritage Report: Carcross Dunes, Carcross Village and Conrad City & District, Department of Renewable Resources, Government of Yukon. 114 pp. 1982.

Coates, Ken. Best Left As Indians: Native-White Relations in the Yukon Territory 1840-1973. Montreal: McGill-Queen's University, 1993.

Coates, Ken and Morrison, William. Land of the Midnight Sun. Montreal: McGill-Queen's University Press, 2005.

Cohen, Stan. The Forgotten War: A Pictorial History of World War II in Alaska and Northeastern Canada. Vols, 1, 2. Missoula: Pictorial Histories Publishing Company, 1981, 1989.

Cohen, Stan. The Trail of '42: A Pictorial History of the Alaska Highway. Missoula: Pictorial Histories Publishing Company, 1979.

Ellis, Pat. Financial Sourdough Starter Stories: The Trump Family, From Whitehorse to the White House, the Klondike Gold Rush, Harry Truman and the A-Bomb. Self-published, 2017.

Ellis, Pat. The Canol Adventures: The Greatest Construction Job Since the Panama Canal. WW II 1942-1945. Gold Island Publishing, 2008.

Firth, John. River Time: Racing the Ghosts of the Klondike Rush. Edmonton: Newest Publishing, 2004.

Gage, S.R. A Walk on the Canol Road. Oakville: Mosaic Press, 1990.

Hare, Greg, with contributions from Sheila Greer (Champagne and Aishihik First Nations), Heather Jones (Carcross/Tagish First Nation), Rae Mombourquette (Kwanlin Dün First Nation), John Fingland (Kluane First Nation). The Frozen Past: The Yukon Ice Patches. Government of Yukon. 48 pp. 2011.

Heller, Ursula. Village Portraits. Toronto: Carswell Legal Publications, 1981.

Jensen, Marilyn. Our Story: A historical reflection of the Carcross/Tagish First Nations land claims process. Carcross: Carcross/Tagish First Nation Ratification Committee, 2005.

Johnson, James A. Carmack of the Klondike. Ganges: Horsdal & Schubart, 1990.

Lundberg, Murray. Fractured Veins & Broken Dreams: Montana Mountain and the Windy Arm Stampede. Whitehorse: Pathfinder Publications, 1997.

Lynch, Jeremiah, Three Years in the Klondike. Chicago: Lakeside Press, 1967.

McClure, Christine and Dennis. We Fought the Road. Kenmore: Epicenter Press, Kenmore, 2017.

Nauske, Claus M. "The Taiya Project." BC Studies. 1991. UBC Library.

Neufeld, David and Norris, Frank. Chilkoot Trail: Heritage Route to the Klondike. Madeira Park: Lost Moose Publishing, 1996.

Porter, C.R. Klondike Paradise. Surrey: Hancock House, 1997.

Rowland, John. Slipping the Lines: Adventures around the World in Peace and War. North Battleford: Turner-Warwick Publications, 1993.

Satterfield, Archie. Chilkoot Pass: Then and Now. Anchorage: Alaska Northwest Publishing, 1973.

Steele, Peter. Atlin's Gold. Prince George: Caitlin Press, 1995.

Taylor, Charles M. Touring Alaska and the Yellowstone. Philadelphia: George W. Jacobs & Co., 1901.

Robb, Jim. The Colourful Five Per Cent Illustrated, Vols. 1, 2, 1984, 1985.

Wells, E. Hazard and Dodd, Randall M. Magnificence and Misery: A Firsthand Account of the 1897 Klondike Gold Rush. Garden City: Doubleday & Co., 1984.

Wilkie, Rab and The Skookum Jim Friendship Centre. Skookum Jim: Native and Non-Native Stories and Views About His Life and Times And the Klondike Gold Rush. Government of Yukon (Heritage Branch, Yukon Tourism), 1992.

Yardley, Joyce. Crazy Cooks and Gold Miners. Surrey: Hancock House, Surrey, 1993.

PHOTO CREDITS

FRONT COVER: *Caribou Hotel painting: Ted Harrison, used with permission from Wingate Arts Limited*

BACK COVER: *Painting by Anna Gertrude Scott, a student of internationally renowned artist Emily Carr. Anna was never in the Yukon yet the parrot, the cage and the background are eerily identical to Polly's residence in the Caribou Hotel. It was believed to have been painted from a photograph in 1948.*

INTERIOR:

McBride Museum of Yukon History - page 3

Anne Morgan postcard collection - page 6

1. Night Visitor: *Anne Morgan - pages 11, 14*

2. The Yukon Hotel: *Yukon Archives, Robert Coutts Fonds (78 69 228) - page 19*
Dawson City Museum (1970 2 1 72) - page 21

3. Todezzane: *Yukon Archives, Anton Vogee Fonds (000058) - page 26*
Dawson City Museum (1998 22 698) - page 27
John Firth - pages 28, 31, 32

4. Big Bill Anderson: *McBride Museum of Yukon History Collection (1999 251 286) - page 36*
Anne Morgan collection (top) - page 37
Yukon Archives, John Scott Fonds (89 31 190)- page 37
John Firth - page 38

5. Importance of Caribou: *John Firth - pages 40, 43*
Dawson City Museum (1984 217 27) - title page, page 42

6. Dawson Charlie: *McBride Museum of Yukon History Collection (1989 1 4) - page 46*
McBride Museum of Yukon History Collection (1999 11 9) - page 48
University of Washington Libraries, Special Collections (39638) - page 50
Michael Nore Collection - page 51

7. Legends Hold Court: *Yukon Archives, Whitehorse Star Ltd Fonds (82 563 f85 46) -*